Appalachian Crossing: The Pocahontas Roads

by

Eugene L. Huddleston

A Photographic and Physiographic Record of the Main Lines of the Chesapeake & Ohio, Norfolk & Western, and Virginian Railways in the Eastern Mountains

ISBN Number: 0-9622003-0-1

Table of Contents

Preface

This little book illustrates the relationship of land forms to the location and operations of what were, until fairly recently, three competing yet complementary railroads whose busy mainlines crossed the southern portion of that often maligned but gloriously beautiful state of West Virginia into the equally scenic state of Virginia. With closely parallel routes and common traffic patterns, these three roads invite joint consideration. For a long time they preserved a distinctive identity in their crossing of the Appalachians. Yet by the mid-1980s, the Chesapeake and Ohio was no longer a viable marking on locomotives and cars, its new name being a trendy initialism—CSX Transportation. The Virginian Railway had been the first to lose its identity, for late in 1959 it was absorbed by the Norfolk and Western, which itself, at about the same time C&O became CSX Transporation, decided its corporate future lay in combination with the Southern, whose slogan "The Southern Serves the South" almost everyone over 50 recalls!

There's no denying that the C&O, Virginian, and N&W shared beautiful scenery and lots of trains, a combination often explored in books and articles. The scenery, however, has been approached as just scenery, with no attempts to classify it or analyze its relationship to the railroads passing through it. If one can label and differentiate the scenery and show what the three railroads have in common with a particular type of scenery, then he can begin to master elements in a photograph that have heretofore been merely bewildering, for finding patterns in something under scrutiny aids in its understanding.

To aid in that understanding, the photos in this book are sequenced west to east and are grouped by physiographic province. Each province is clearly delineated by distinctive land-form characteristics which are explained in the introduction and classified relative to the railroads passing through them in the one table in that chapter. On topographical maps placed near the railroad and region under consideration, one can find town names and other features of the landscape that identify the approximate boundaries of each physiographic region for each railroad. The gradient profiles also offer a key to the railroad's relation to a particular region as well as a basis of comparison for how each railroad copes with the mountain barriers each must contend with.

Photos of the three railroads are kept separate in each region, except for the Virginian and Norfolk and Western in the Valley and Ridge Province, where the two roads ran for most of the distance on opposite banks of the New River. (After the late-1960s some duplicate trackage was eliminated by demolishing the big Virginian bridge at Glen Lyn and constructing a new and smaller one just east of Narrows, Virginia.) Every region is represented by at least one photo from each road, except for the Virginian in the Blue Ridge Province. Because the Virginian followed the course of the Roanoke River and its tributary, Goose Creek, through the Blue Ridge barrier (and because the range at this point is not very scenic), few photographers "shot" the Virginian mainline just east of Roanoke. Photographers were more captivated by N&W's crossing of the Blue Ridge a few miles north, which involved steam locomotives longer, more scenery, greater accessibility by rail and highway, more traffic, and heavier grades. Possibly the only really scenic spot on the old Virginian between Roanoke and Altavista (where the mainline rejoins the Roanoke River) is between Stone Mountain and Huddleston Tunnel, where the single track-line, emerging from the tunnel, almost immediately crosses Goose Creek. (Since the 1960s this portion of the old Virginian has been the eastbound main track for the N&W — or Norfolk Southern — with the former N&W main farther north serving as the westbound track.)

While the geographical scope of the photo coverage can be clearly delineated, the chronological coverage cannot be as clearly fixed or as logically approached. The photos date from the mid-1940s to the 1980s, with the decade of the 1950s predominating. It was in the 1950s that steam gave way to diesels as motive power, roughly 1956 for the C&O, 1959 for the N&W, and 1955 for the Virginian. The Virginian's mainline electrification between Mullens and Roanoke, however, did not give way to dieselization until June 30, 1962, 2-1/2 years following the N&W-Virginian merger in 1959. Determining the ordering of the three roads in the book is the number of illustrations available for each road.

INTRODUCTION

Mountain scenery delights and inspires. Few other forms of nature can so readily evoke in the beholder the sense of the sublime. For many, putting trains into the scene intensifies the delight even more. Many spots in the Appalachian mountain chain illustrate this appeal. For example, truly sublime is the spot above West Point, New York, where the wide and placid Hudson flows between the brows of four looming mountains— Storm King and Crow's Nest on the west and Break Neck and Bull Hill on the east. This magnificent panorama is seen to best advantage from Inspiration Point on the grounds of the U. S. Military Academy. But making the prospect even more appealing are the former New York Central lines (now Conrail) along both banks of the river—the former four-track main on the east side and the now busier West Shore line. Or, at the opposite end of the Appalachian chain, one looks down from the park at the top of Lookout Mountain upon the grand vista of the city of Chattanooga, the Cumberland Plateau, and Moccasin Bend of the Tennessee River, where the Southern (now Norfolk Southern) winds along its banks far below the viewer.

Railroads fit in so well with the natural beauty of the Appalachian landscapes that one is not surprised to discover that artists who are not "rail buffs" have put trains or locomotives into their landscapes to enhance their appeal. In his book *The Machine in the Garden*, Leo Marx explained how in the nineteenth century the train became a metaphor for progress and natural scenery a metaphor for primitivism, two conflicting forces in American intellectual history. That artists in the nineteenth century could introduce trains into a natural landscape indicated to Marx that for a time American culture was balanced between a need to preserve the past and to move into the future. Trains, which seemed almost alive, could represent the positive side of industrial technology. Thus was achieved a Golden Mean between the extreme democratic and uncivilized wilderness on the one hand and of crowded cities and class-conscious factories on the other. In both George Inness' "The Lackawanna Valley" (1855) and Jasper Cropsey's "Starucca Viaduct" (1865), the vast and peaceful landscapes are "home" for the steam-powered train coursing through it, and each painter has captured both this harmony and the sublimity of the natural scenery. With ever increasing industrialization in the twentieth century no longer were such balanced landscapes possible. Yet many a railroad enthusiast would argue that the possibility of harmonizing trains with the natural landscape did not die with the nineteenth century, for such harmony will be achievable as long as there are mountains and steel rails running through them. "Harmony" is perhaps not quite the right word; "sublime" perhaps better characterizes the mating of the awe-inspiring aspects of nature with the equally awesome power of the locomotive!

Besides railroads and mountains going hand in hand in cultural symbolism, they go together historically; that is, they literally illustrate the clash between progress and primitivism in the movement of American civilization westward. For railroads developed as the culmination of attempts to open the interior to development by conquering the chief obstacle to westward travel—the Appalachian chain. First came Daniel Boone and the "Wilderness Trail," then the canals, most notably the Erie, and finally the railroads. George Washington, wanting to keep the West away from the influence of the British and sensing the potential for the enormous future growth of America, early started looking for paths through the Appalachians connecting his native Virginia with the interior—specifically the Ohio Valley and Great Lakes territory.

While encamped at Newburgh, New York, in 1783 (the year of the peace treaty with Britain), Washington had traveled up the Mohawk and was delighted to discover how easily developed would be this route to Lake Erie and the West. But it was his native Virginia that he was most interested in seeing developed commercially, so almost as soon as he was freed of his military duties he made a trip to discover the best possible canal and portage routes west over the Appalachians. On this 1784 trip he learned of three practical routes: up the North Branch of the Potomac and thence over the divide into the valley of the Little Youghiogheny; from the Jackson's River (headwaters of the James) up Dunlap's Creek and thence over the divide to Howard's Creek, the Greenbrier, the New, and Great Kanawha; and up the Roanoke (in the Great or Shenandoah Valley) over the divide to the New and thence to the Holston or the Great Kanawha.

Washington was not much impressed with the Roanoke route, for even though there was only a fairly low divide between this river and the New (the same route now used by both the former Virginian and N&W routes of the Norfolk Southern) the Roanoke flowed out of Virginia into the state of North Carolina. The James and the Potomac were the only rivers a native Virginian could consider, and Washington made this clear in a letter to John Filson, Kentucky writer and explorer, on January 15, 1785: "That the river Potomac communicates by short portages . . . with the Yohoghaney {sic} and Cheat Rivers . . . for the countries East and West of the Appalachian mountains, as James River also does with the Waters of the Great Kanwha {sic}, none can deny, and that these will be the channels thro' which the trade of the Western country will principally come, I have no more doubt of myself, than the states of Virginia and Maryland had, when within these few days, they have passed laws for the purpose of extending and improving the navigation of these rivers, and opening roads of communication between them and the Western waters."

While both the Potomac and James routes westward were both important to the state of Virginia, the James-Kanawha route was more truly Virginian than the Potomac-Youghiogheny because Richmond, principal city and capital, was on the James. Alexandria was the only town of significance on the Potomac, which at that time had as much importance to Marylanders as to Virginians. Some 40 years later, Claudius Crozet, emigre French army officer and Principal Engineer for the Virginia Board of Public Works, surveyed "practicable" (in his words) canal and railroad routes to the west for the state. He reported that two rail routes were feasible, both having the same advantage: "from the head of the valley of . . . James River, or of Roanoke, there is only one ridge to be passed over; after which, the Valley of New River may be pursued down to the Ohio."

Crozet proved remarkably prescient, for almost half a century later, the Chesapeake and Ohio appropriated essentially the same James-to-New River route; the Norfolk and Western, a little later than C&O, came to the New by way of Roanoke, but left the New long before its confluence with the Great Kanawha. The N&W might certainly have proceeded down the New to the Kanawha and thence to the Ohio but for two reasons: the C&O, protecting both banks of the New, had already appropriated this route, and most importantly the N&W had left the New to follow the East River, a tributary on the edge of the Appalachian Plateau, to the

Great Flat Top coal fields. Eventually N&W would reach the Ohio, but not by a route a locating engineer would have picked for ease of grades and curvature; rather a circuitous route over FlatTtop Mountain and down the Tug Fork, Big Sandy, and Ohio was about the only choice N&W had for constructing west out of the coal fields. Compensating, of course, for this almost continuously curving line was access to even more seams of coal-rich southern West Virginia.

The Virginian Railway, unlike C&O and N&W, was constructed out of the coal fields to the east coast. Because it originally offered only a route east and that one redundant with C&O's and N&W's own routes to Tidewater, the Virginian, perhaps, should never have been built. From one perspective, the Virginian was built out of spite. Financier Henry Huttleston Rogers was determined not to be done in by the collusion of the New York Central under William K. Vanderbilt and the Pennsylvania under Alexander Cassett. These bold capitalists, in a "community of interests" pact, gained control of both the N&W and C&O. Their goal was, through introducing a monopoly into the transportation of bituminous coal, to dictate rates. (Initially, anti-trust legislation did not apply to railroads.) Rogers was thus frustrated in attempting to get a fair pro-rated cut of the revenue from coal originating on his Deepwater Railroad for shipment east over either C&O or N&W. He therefore spent 40 million dollars of his own money to build his own outlet to the port of Hampton Roads on Chesapeake Bay. Upon completion of this well-engineered road in 1909 Rogers died. Its route closely paralleled the N&W's. Both roads had to climb to the top of Flat Top Mountain and both utilized the East River to descend from the Plateau to the level of the New River. Additionally both utilized the New (the Virginian on the north, or east, bank and the N&W on the south) from approximately the West Virginia-Virginia state line to just north of Radford, where both headed east over the single divide separating the New from the Roanoke basin; that is, the Great Valley.

Common to all three of these roads was that appeal possessed by railroads in mountainous country: the awe-inspiring display of power of the locomotives assigned to climb over those mountains! This power manifested itself most spectacularly in the jet-like exhaust blasts reverberating from hillside to hillside emitted by giants of the rails like the N&W Y-6b and the C&O H-8. Somewhat less spectacular is the diesel, yet its intense sound of efficient power under full control can still excite the observer. One must admit, however, that aside from the novelty of the straight electric locomotive, there is little to rivet one's attention to it. One might smell ozone around, say, the Virginian streamlined EL-2B, but the only sound to speak of would be the electric motor blowers.

Of the three competing roads, the Norfolk and Western had overall the severest and lengthiest grades. Although the Virginian's route paralleled the N&W's, it was built about 28 years later, and hence its engineering was more advanced; e.g., new construction techniques permitted cuts and fills of greater magnitude. Chesapeake and Ohio had the easiest grades of all three by far because it did not have to climb over the Appalachian Plateau to get through it, as did the Virginian and N&W, and it has a water-level route—the Jackson and James Rivers—through a large part of the Valley and Ridge Province and entirely through the Blue Ridge.

By no means did these three roads exceed others in the East in either steepness of grades or even in volume of traffic. Take the former Baltimore and Ohio and Western Maryland lines, for example. On the B&O's Cumberland-Pittsburgh line, the climb up the Appalachian Front (eastern escarpment of the Appalachian Plateau) to Sand Patch Tunnels involved a sustained grade of 2.25 percent. And the famous Seventeen-Mile Grade on the Cumberland-Parkersburg line, also ascending the Appalachian Front, is a tortuous 2.5 percent from Piedmont, West Virginia, on the North Branch of the Potomac, to Altamont, Maryland, on top of the Plateau. The eastward ascent of the Plateau on this line is even more impressive, however, because of the heavy movements of coal up and over it. This 11.7 miles of 2.2 percent, from M&K Jct. on the Cheat River to Terra Alta, West Virginia, has a name evoking instant recognition: the Cranberry.

The severest grade of any line in the East crossing the Appalachians was that facing eastbound coal tonnage from Hendricks to Thomas, West Virginia: 11 miles ranging from 2 percent to 2.9 percent, with the last two miles being 3.5 percent. The only proviso here, however, is that only loosely could this now-abandoned ascent of the Plateau, on the line from Elkins, West Virginia, to Cumberland, Maryland, be called a <u>main</u> line. On the "true" main line of the Western Maryland—the Connellsville to Baltimore line—was the highest main line crossing of the whole range of the Appalachians: 3,060 feet above sea level at Deal, Pennsylvania, also now abandoned. (The maximum altitude of any main line on the three Pocahontas roads was on the Norfolk and Western at Bluefield, West Virginia: 2,567 feet.)

That the grades on the B&O and Western Maryland exceeded, overall, those of the C&O, N&W, and Virginian is easily demonstrated. The C&O could hardly even enter the contest for the steepest and longest grades. Granted, the Mountain Subdivision, which served as the main line for through passenger trains, had grades of up to 1.5 percent in crossing (by passes) several ridges of the Valley and Ridge Province and in climbing to a tunnel through the Blue Ridge. However, the main route west of the Mountain line for both freight and passenger trains was the Alleghany Subdivision, which reached the summit of the Atlantic-Gulf watershed at 2,072 feet above sea level and a ruling grade of only .57 percent eastbound and 1.14 percent westbound. The Norfolk and Western's longest and steepest mainline grade was up Elkhorn Creek from Welch to the tunnel under Great Flat Top Mountain, a Monadnock—that is, a singular peak or ridge rising above the surface of the lifted peneplain, in this case the Appalachian Plateau. Here the ruling grade against eastbound coal is nine miles of 1.4 percent. (In 1915 this grade was electrified, but with construction of a new, larger tunnel on slightly lowered gradient in 1950, steam was brought back!) The Virginian also climbed to the top of Flat Top Mountain, but 10 miles north of the N&W and up a twelve-mile grade which reaches 2.07 percent. This grade, too, was electrified but not until 1925. The N&W, which absorbed the Virginian in 1959, ended electrification in 1962—catenary which had extended for 131 miles from Mullens, West Virginia (Elmore yard) to Roanoke. Both N&W and Virginian managed to escape major grades for their eastbound coal moving over the Blue Ridge barrier, the N&W by a wind gap and the Virginian by a water gap. There were, and are, other significant grades in the East created by the Appalachian Mountain barrier, but few of them had the tonnage moving over them as did the B&O, the Western Maryland, and the three Pocahontas roads. (The Clinchfield, or as it was early known—the Carolina, Clinchfield, and Ohio--also crossed the Appalachians, but most of its coal tunnage moved north, away from the mountain barriers.) One eastern road, however, the huge Pennsylvania system, did have more tonnage moving across the mountains than any of the West Virginia coal roads. Its four-track main ascended the eastern escarpment of the Appalachian Plateau just west of Altoona, Pennsylvania, gaining altitude by the famous Horseshoe Curve on a ruling grade of 1.75 percent, which calculated for curvature increased to 2.1 percent. This steep grade was not matched by the eastbound grade, for it ascended the Plateau quite gradually, mostly by the valley of the Conemaugh River.

A word of caution needs to be added here. Some of the big grades in the East no longer exist. Especially have mergers of parallel roads, like the Western Maryland and B&O and the Virginian and N&W, led to the steepest grades being abandoned or downgraded wherever possible. Mountain divisions are obviously more expensive to operate than those in level territory. And retrenchments continue; it is only a matter of time until the C&O's scenic and historically important Mountain Subdivision is abandoned.

While the Appalachian crossings of the three Pocahontas roads may not have exceeded those of others in the East in either grades or tonnage, they did exceed the others in grandeur and variety of scenery. And giving to them an unusual unity was the commonality of physiography in the regions all three traversed. The regions, from west to east, were the Appalachian (or Alleghany) Plateau, the Valley and Ridge, the Great Valley of Virginia, and the Blue Ridge. Together these four regions comprise the Appalachian Chain. The *Guide to West Virginia*, sponsored by the West Virginia Writers' Project of the WPA, explains well the characteristics of these regions within the state:

> The State is divided into two physiographic provinces by an escarpment known as the Allegheny Front, which extends in an irregular line from Keyser, on the West Virginia-Maryland boundary, southwestward to Bluefield, on the West Virginia-Virginia line. East of the Front is the Appalachian Valley and Ridge Province. The drainage of this portion of West Virginia . . . is of the trellis pattern characteristic of such strongly folded areas. Weathering and erosion have etched into bold relief . . . {the folded and upturned} massive sandstone strata and at the same time have created valleys in the weaker limestones and shales. In this manner parallel ridges and valleys have been formed, with a general northeast-southwest trend. Some streams flow in a trough or valley for 40 or 50 miles, cross a ridge through a water gap, and then resume the original direction in a parallel valley. The rectangular pattern thus formed is known as trellis drainage. . . West of the Front, covering an area of more than 20,000 square miles, is a part of the Appalachian Plateau Province known as the Allegheny Plateau. The drainage of the Allegheny Plateau is dendritic (treelike), a type of drainage occurring where rock strata are nearly horizontal and the guidance of the streams is slight. The drainage waters of this part of the state eventually reach the Ohio River.

Since Virginia is east of West Virginia, the Valley and Ridge Province naturally extends into Virginia. One can note generally the trend of the ridges and valleys by examining on a map the West Virginia-Virginia state line. From the eastern panhandle to Bluefield, the line roughly marks the westernmost ridge of the Province. The eastern edge of the Province (roughly about four major parallel ridges wide) can be approximated by again looking at a map: Interstate 81 runs approximately down the middle of the Great Valley (also commonly known as the Shenandoah Valley), which varies from five to 25 miles in width. This "valley" hardly exhibits the uniform flatness most associated with valleys; rather, it is rolling and hilly. Making this depression a valley is the last long parallel ridge on the west (the Alleghanies) and on the east, the Blue Ridge, composed of rock much older than in the Valley and Ridge province and much more complex in structure. Its ridges are apt to be more irregular than the ridges of the Alleghanies, and typically it is only one ridge wide. East of the Blue Ridge there are no real mountains, only the "foothills" of the Blue Ridge, which mark the western boundary of the Piedmont section of Virginia.

Table 1 indicates how one can determine what segments of the three Pocahontas roads are in each particular region and identifies briefly the distinguishing characteristics of each region. By this point it should be clear that the main lines of the three Pocahontas roads have much in common: frequent and heavy-tonnage coal trains and routes connecting Chesapeake Bay with the Ohio Valley. (While the Virginian did not directly reach the Ohio Valley, it did indirectly through the western connection of

TABLE 1. -- PHYSIOGRAPHIC PROVINCES

REGION (from west to east)	IDENTIFYING CHARACTERISTICS	APPROXIMATE BOUNDARIES (west to east and by station)		
		C&O	N&W	VIRGINIAN
APPALACHIAN PLATEAU	Level, uplifted surface dissected by streams in dendritic (leaf) pattern; sedimentary rocks exposed in horizontal bedding.	Chillicothe (Hopetown), OH, and Morehead, KY, to Talcott (Big Bend Tunnel), WV.	Chilllicothe, OH, to Glen Lyn, VA and Batavia, OH, to Glen Lyn.	Deepwater Bridge and Gilbert, WV (farthest point west) to Glen Lyn, VA.
VALLEY AND RIDGE	High parallel ridges with generally level ridge lines and streams in trellis pattern; sedimentary and metamorphic rocks are folded and exposed in cuts at various angles.	Alderson, WV to North Mountain, VA and Alderson to Buchanan, VA.	Narrows, VA to Elliston, VA.	Narrows, VA to Ironto, VA.
GREAT VALLEY	Wide, often rolling or hilly depression between easternmost ridge of Valley and Ridge Province and the Blue Ridge barrier.	From just west of Staunton (Snyder), VA to just east of Waynesboro (Basic), VA and from Natural Bridge to Balcony Falls (Glasgow).	From just east of Elliston, VA to just east of Roanoke (Bonsack), VA.	From just east of Ironto, VA to just east of Roanoke (Hardy), VA.
BLUE RIDGE	High, irregular ridge lines; metamorphic and igneous rocks in complex structures; typically one massive ridge in width.	Waynesboro (Basic), VA to Crozet, VA and Balcony Falls to Big Island.	Bonsack, VA to Bedford, VA.	(ill-defined boundaries) from approx. Stewartsville, VA to Stone Mountain, VA.

its main line with the New York Central at Deepwater Bridge, West Virginia.)

Even more impressively similar was the common geography and physiography of the three main lines. The federal government recognized this overall commonality when it took over operation of the nation's railroads in World War I. When American railroads collectively and literally broke down during the winter of 1917-1918, the President created the United States Railroad Administration to coordinate operations and eliminate traffic tie-ups and equipment shortages. In January 1918, each railroad was assigned a geographic region under a regional manager. Originally assigned to the Eastern, the C&O, N&W, and Virginian were given their own region when, on June 1, 1918, the Eastern Region was subdivided into the Eastern, Allegheny and Pocahontas Regions. The Pocahontas, headquartered in Roanoke, Virginia, included the C&O east of Columbus and Cincinnati, plus the entire N&W and Virginian. Although a relatively small region, these railroads were immensely important in handling the nation's fuel supply. Even after the War, when the nation's railroads were returned to their owners, these roads, along with the Clinchfield, continued to be classified as Pocahontas carriers for purposes of financial analysis and statistical reporting.

Another significant aspect of the history of the mountain crossings of the Pocahontas roads was the named passenger trains formerly plying the main lines. The Virginian, of course, had no named passenger trains because its main line paralleled the N&W's, which had already captured whatever passenger potential existed in the hinterlands and also because the Virginian connected no large cities: the best it could do was Norfolk, Virginia, with Charleston, West Virginia. C&O's line across the Appalachians reached the largest cities of the three: through Pullman service from New York to St. Louis and Louisville. So much did C&O's premier train, *The George Washington*, represent the *espirit* of the railroad company that any employee responsible for delaying this train would be subject to payless leaves from work, even dismissal from service, no matter what the excuse. But alas for railfans! The *George,* being principally a Pullman train, ran at night in both directions. Only because it ran late once in a while are there any photos of it crossing the Appalachians. The same night-time scheduling applies to the N&W's former premier train, *The Pocahontas.* But one fine N&W train, established soon after the end of World War II, did run in the daytime through the mountains—*The Powhatan Arrow* (This completely new daylight streamliner was named after Pocahontas's father by an N&W employee, who won a contest to name the new train.) *The Chessie,* C&O's version of *The Powhatan Arrow*, never went into service, even though lightweight equipment and special locomotives for the new train had been received and went on display system-wide in 1948.

The N&W and C&O both had other named trains. The C&O's *Sportsman* ran from Detroit to Norfolk and enjoyed good patronage, especially during World War II. Luckily for rail photographers, it ran through the mountains both ways mostly in daylight. The *F.F.V.* ("Fast Flying Virginian" or "First Families of Virginia"?) from Cincinnati to Washington traversed both ways only the New River Gorge both directions in daylight. On the N&W *The Cavalier* was a glorified local which traversed the territory west of Bluefield in daylight. After the inauguration of Amtrak in 1971 and the discontinuance of all the above-named trains, there was then, as now, only one train crossing the Appalachians. Initially named *The James Whitcomb Riley* after a former NYC train, it ran from Chicago to Washington (and Newport News) via the NYC (Big Four) and C&O, mostly at night through the mountains. For a few years in the late 1970s, *The Mountaineer* ran over the N&W from Norfolk to Kenova and thence to a connection with *The Cardinal* at Catlettsburg, Kentucky. (*The James Whitcomb Riley* name had been dropped after a route change through Indiana.) At the time they were in service together, both were night trains through the mountains. At the time of this writing, the *Cardinal* runs every other day, but traverses the scenic areas mostly in the daylight. *The Mountaineer* was eliminated late in 1979.

Comparative Profiles

(See Page 7)

These three gradient profiles were prepared in 1924 when C&O was making its case before the Interstate Commerce Commission for control of the Virginian. The profiles are still mostly accurate in the 1980s. However, portions of the Virginian line have been downgraded or combined with the N&W main line. Also, the summit of "Elkhorn Mountain" has been lowered about 100 feet by a 1950 construction project. A new double-track tunnel, more than 6,900 feet long, replaced the single-track Elkhorn Tunnel, 3,014 feet long, under Great Flat Top Mountain. One major summit is common to all three profiles—the summit marking the watershed between the Atlantic Ocean and the Mississippi River. On C&O this summit was at Alleghany, Virginia; on the N&W near Christiansburg; and on the Virginian at Merrimac, Virginia. The heaviest grades on the Virginian and N&W were on the ascent to the top of the Appalachian Plateau (Clarks Gap on the Virginian and Elkhorn Tunnel on the N&W). The profiles disclose that C&O had the easiest gradients from the coal fields to Chesapeake Bay (port of Hampton Roads). C&O did not have to ascend the Appalachian Plateau, for the New River cut through it; further, by following the banks of the Jackson and James River (the latter a former canal route), C&O was able to avoid climbing the Blue Ridge, which the James penetrated by a water gap at Snowden, Virginia. N&W crossed the Blue Ridge via a wind gap, making for a fairly mild grade, considering the ruggedness of the range otherwise. Virginian, like C&O, adhered to a water gap made by the Roanoke River in the Blue Ridge, up to a point, that is; for the Virginian left the main valley of the Roanoke east of Roanoke to follow one of its tributaries, Goose Creek, for several miles.

The fourth profile shows the C&O's Mountain Subdivision, which was its main passenger route east to west. This line contrasts greatly with the James River line, which it roughly parallels. It is so mountainous, in fact, that C&O successor CSX Transportation in the 1980s made plans to abandon it. Not only did this line have to cross the Blue Ridge (east of Waynesboro, Virginia, at Blue Ridge Tunnel) but it also had to cross a major ridge of the Valley and Ridge Province—at Great North Mountain. A shorter grade west of Goshen took the line through another great ridge of this province via a water gap named Panther Gap.

6

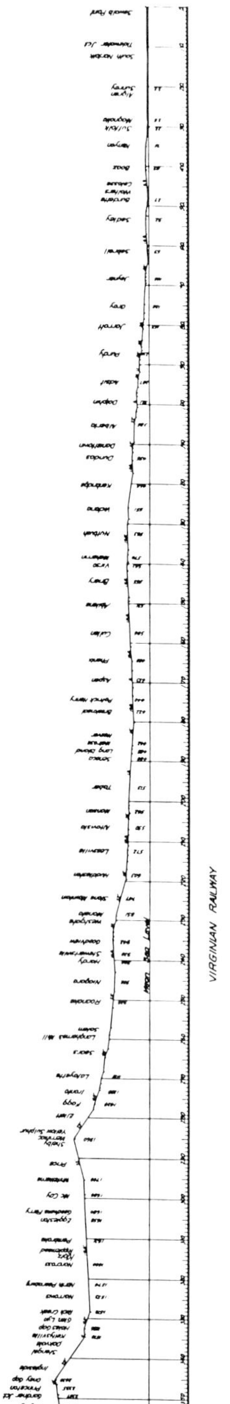

VIRGINIAN RAILWAY
CHESAPEAKE AND OHIO RAILWAY 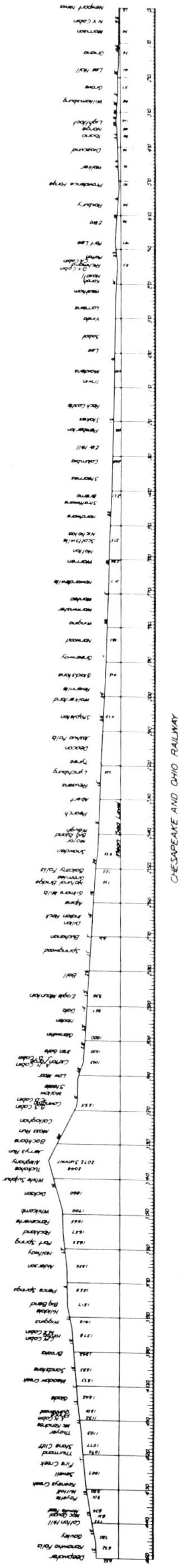
NORFOLK AND WESTERN RAILWAY 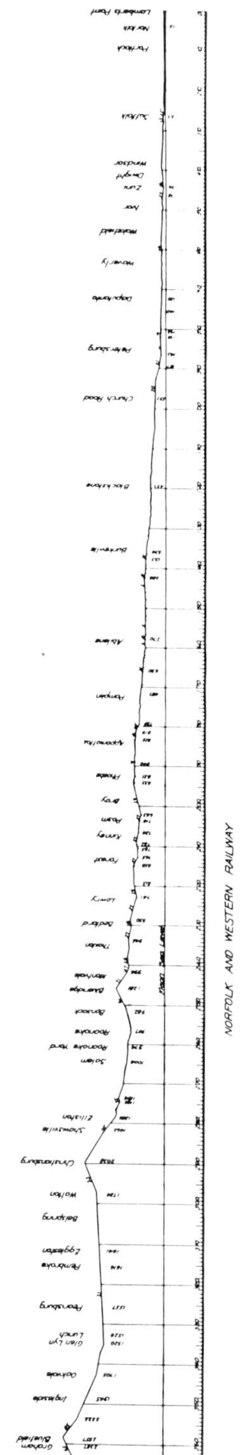

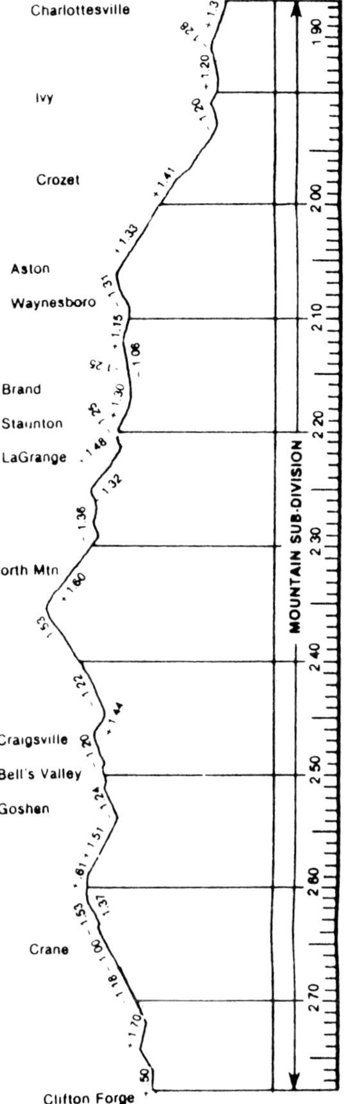

Charlottesville
Ivy
Crozet
Aston
Waynesboro
Brand
Staunton
LaGrange
North Mtn
Craigsville
Bell's Valley
Goshen
Crane
Clifton Forge
MOUNTAIN SUB-DIVISION
190
200
210
220
230
240
250
260
270

Chapter I

The Chesapeake and Ohio Railway

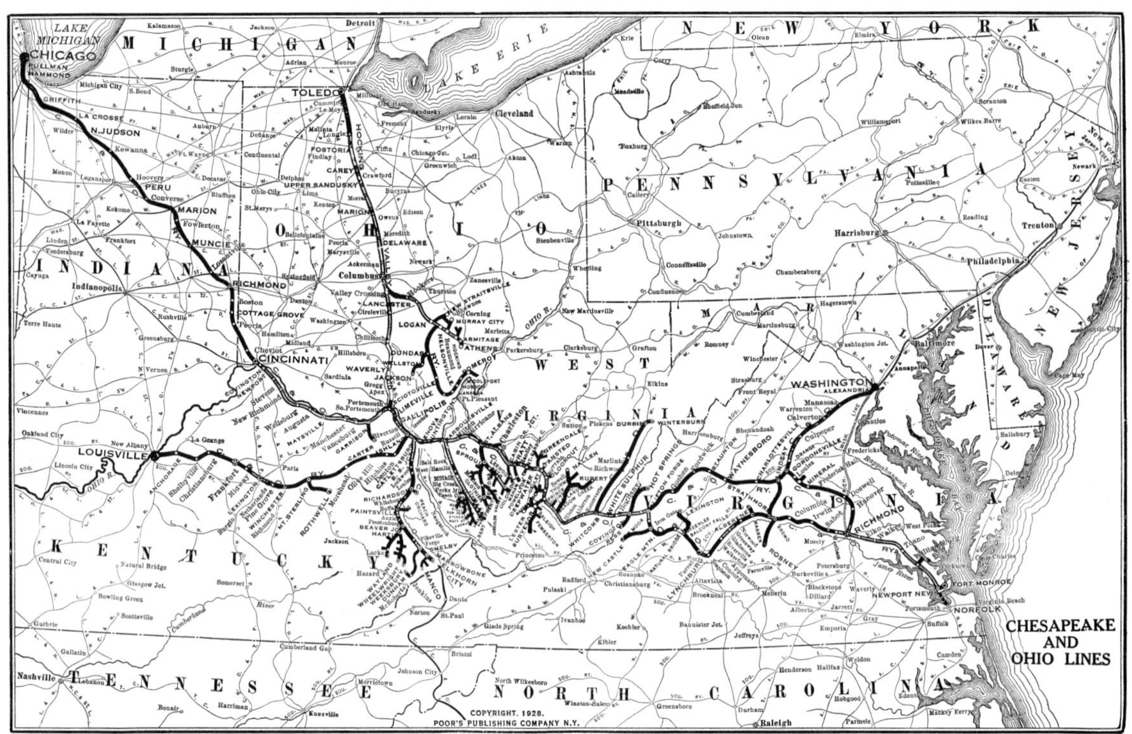

C&O System map taken from 1928 edition of *Poor's Manual of the Railroads*

In The Appalachian Plateau

In Ohio, the western boundary of the Plateau is marked by the southernmost spread of great glaciers that long ago flattened the landscapes over which they passed. The most extensive province of the four comprising the Appalachian Crossing is the Appalachian (or Alleghany) Plateau, also called Appalachia.

With the camera aimed southward in August 1988, a CSXT coal train bound for Columbus crosses the Pickaway Plains south of Circleville. The hill visible in the left background is Mount Logan, featured on the Great Seal of Ohio. The line of hills of which Mount Logan is a part rises suddenly from the gentle glaciated topography of the Central Lowlands and forms the western escarpment of the Appalachian Plateau. Although the "climb" over the Appalachians does not begin here, the effect of the plateau in determining railroad locations does.

Gene Huddleston

The same train headed by 6717 bound from Russell to Columbus, seen looking north on the Pickaway Plains south of Circleville. The glaciation is evident in the leveled landscape though some variety is accorded by the hummocky rises against the skyline. Power on this coal train includes a GP40, a B30-7, and a rare General Electric former Seaboard BQ23-7.

Gene Huddleston

As strange as it may seem, the hills in the background of the photo of 6717 mark a major boundary in American geography. To the northwest of these hills stretch plains all the way to the Rockies. Behind these hills, to the southeast, are the hills of the Appalachian Plateau and mountains beyond the hills!

At Russell, Kentucky, in August 1978, surrounded by the hills of the Appalachian Plateau, former Reading 4-8-4 No. 2101 leaves late in the afternoon for Columbus with a heavily loaded excursion train. The handsome Northern will make good time running over the level flood plain of the Ohio River as far as Limeville.

Gene Huddleston

Hidden by the trees at right is the Ohio River, which this C&O train to the coal fields will follow to one of its tributaries—either the Big Sandy, Little or Big Coal, or the Kanawha. In this 1947 view just east of Russell, the motive power is a class H-5 2-6-6-2, built for the United States Railroad Administration in 1919.

Gene Huddleston

9

Gene Huddleston

This 1953 view of empties heading back to the Virginian connection at West Gilbert gives a fair idea of how, if one gets far enough back, he can see that the summits of the hills in Appalachia form a mostly *level* skyline. Across the river is Ohio; the train is in Kentucky (Catlettsburg) but will soon cross the Big Sandy into West Virginia.

As trains head east through the Appalachian Plateau, they follow rivers—the Ohio, Kanawha and New principally. Or else they follow the bed of a pre-glacial ancestor of the Ohio, the Teays.

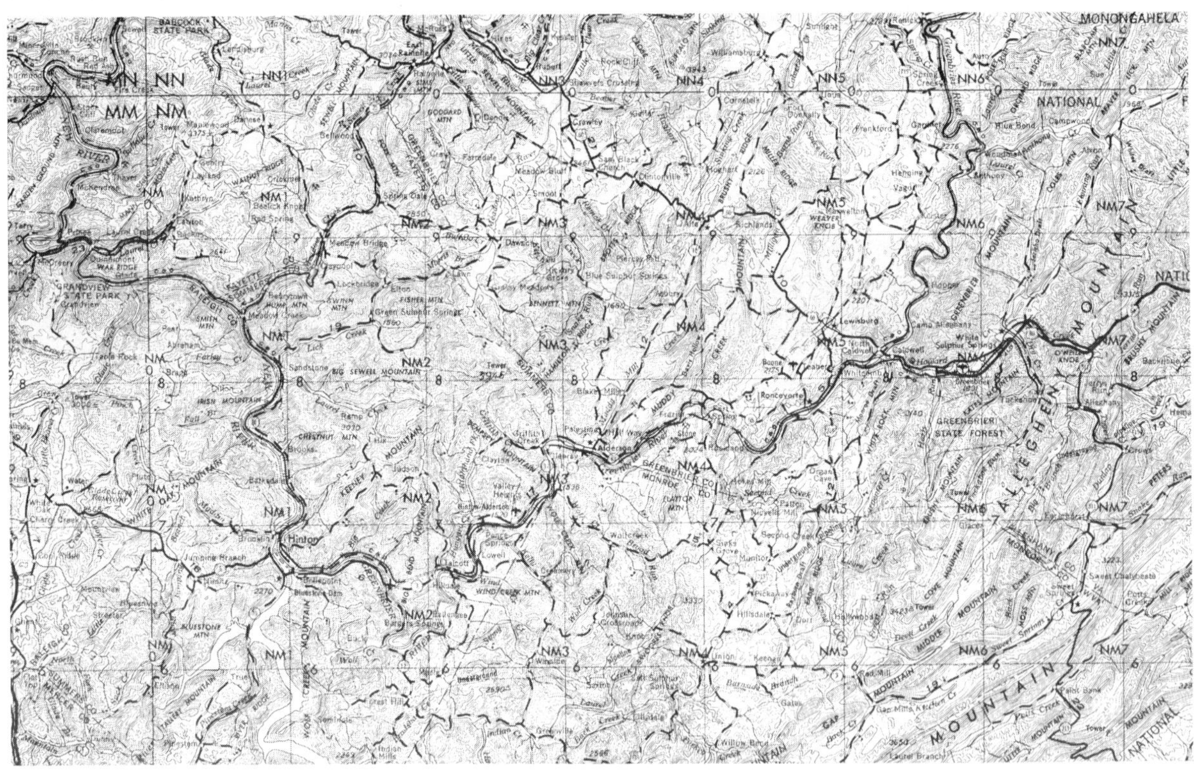

The focus of map A is the C&O mainline from the heart of the New River Gorge over the Alleghanies almost to Clifton Forge. The railroad leaves the Appalachian Plateau roughly at *Talcott* (at east portal of Big Bend Tunnel, clearly discernable on map). From Talcott east are mostly rolling limestone uplands to *Caldwell*, where the true mountains begin. From Caldwell, then, to *Backbone* is the most scenic and operationally interesting portion of the line. Alleghany Tunnel (twin bores) under the state line is seen just under the letter "E" in ALLEGHENY MOUNTAIN. Of the twelve tunnels on this portion of the mainline few can be clearly seen. Most of the tunnels in the Plateau (e.g., Stretchers Neck at *Prince* and Big Bend) avoid long bends in the New and Greenbrier Rivers. (Editor's Note: A note should be made here on the spelling of Alleghany. We have spelled it consistently throughout this book with an "a" — Alleghany. This is the old Virginia

10

spelling of the Indian word which means "endless." However, most people spell it with an "e" — Allegheny, because this is the way it appears on most maps, and is a spelling of the mountain range used in the North, where most modern maps were made. The designers of the C&O's huge 2-6-6-6 type intended to name the locomotive for the grade that it challenged, but being mid-westerners at the Cleveland headquarters of the Van Sweringen railroad conglomerate, they spelled it "Allegheny." Therefore, you can have an "Allegheny" type locomotive on the Alleghany subdivision of the C&O on Alleghany Mountain! - This map spells the mountain with an "e", as is typical. There are yet other ways to spell the word, such as "Allegany", which is current in western Maryland.

C&O Historical Society Collection; by Gene Huddleston

C&O follows major rivers from Cincinnati to the base of the Alleghany Mountain crossing. The one exception is the Teays Valley (the valley being named after this settlement), which the railroad follows overland between Huntington and St. Albans, West Virginia. The Teays was a major river before the age of the great glaciers. The westbound freight shown here in 1958 is running over the abandoned bed of the Teays, in a valley about as wide as the Ohio Valley.

Gene Huddleston

The banks of rivers in Appalachia provided the only practical location for the railroads crossing the Plateau region. Behind class H-6 2-6-6-2 No. 1510 at Handley, West Virginia, is the Kanawha River, which empties into the Ohio at Point Pleasant, West Virginia, and which itself is formed by the junction of the Gauley and New Rivers about 20 miles upstream from Handley.

Since the C&O first built through this spot in 1872, its appearance has been much altered. Originally, "Shoo Fly" Tunnel near Gauley penetrated the huge sandstone conglomerate cliff in the background and there was barely room for a single track on the ledge blasted out. By the time of this photo in 1956, the right-of-way had been considerably widened by fill material.

Gene Huddleston

The New River Gorge

C&O Ry; C&O Historical Society Collection

Giving away that this photo was made in the Appalachian Plateau is the nearly horizontal bedding of the rocks—in this case, shale and sandstone, not very resistant to weathering. Extra 1626 East is near Cotton Hill, West Virgina in 1947.

From the Kanawha, C&O follows New River as far as Hinton where it then follows the Greenbrier. C&O is thus able to penetrate the Appalachian Plateau by river level grades. Hawks Nest rock, at right, is 585 feet above the level of New River. Train is No. 92, eastbound, in 1947.

C&O Ry; C&O Historical Society Collection

Eastbound coal train blasts up the New River over a .38 percent grade, not compensated for curvature. Top of cliff in background, across the river, is 1,100 feet above the water. Double-track main is split through this portion of the gorge, one track on each side of the river. This class H-8 is near Kaymoor, West Virginia, in 1947, on the south side of New River.

C&O Ry; C&O Historical Society Collection

The New has cut through the Appalachian Plateau in a spectacular fashion. Here at Whitcomb's Boulder, a mile east of Fayette Station, West Virginia, Amtrak's *The Cardinal* winds up river at about 55 mph February 23, 1986. C&O's second main line shows through the trees across the river.

John Joseph

Amtrak No. 50, the eastbound *Cardinal*, on its first scheduled daylight run through the Gorge April 29, 1984, passes under the four-lane arch bridge completed in 1978 as part of the Appalachian corridor highway program. The highway surface is a towering 876 feet above the New River, which is hidden by foliage at left.

John Joseph

Yes, a caboose is down there—a yellow one behind an eastbound coal train slowly ascending the New on the south mainline, across the river from Keeney's Creek Jct., in March 1986. This spectacular gorge of the New permits C&O to go through the Plateau rather than climb over it.

Gene Huddleston

14

The men on the tender of this Consolidation have had a scenic view in their ride through the New River Gorge from the Keeney's Creek switchback (which their train had to descend) to the west end of Thurmond yard, where the photo was taken in 1953. A twin Consolidation, ahead of the caboose, is on the other end of the train.

C&O Historical Society; by Gene Huddleston

In the "classic" days of C&O railroading, Hinton was an important terminal lying a few miles from the eastern edge of the Appalachian Plateau and the western edge of the Valley and Ridge section. The "mountains" in the background, if seen from the summits, would present a level surface, evidence of the eroded Plateau. The ex-Lehigh Valley 2-10-2 and the U.S.R.A. 2-6-6-2 are on their way to eastern Virginia from the Huntington Locomotive Shops running light after being overhauled and repainted in July 1948.

C&O Historical Society Collection; by Gene Huddleston

Mail-express train No. 104 leaves Hinton for Clifton Forge in July 1948. Cliff at right is composed of the so-called Hinton sandstone. Coal dock (unused) was built especially to supply the eastbound *Chessie* powered by one of the three M-1 steam-turbine-electrics, Nos. 500-502. Fog hangs low in the New River Valley.

Gene Huddleston

In order to get passenger power from Hinton back to Clifton Forge, this J-3 4-8-4 No. 601 has been assigned as pusher to an eastbound coal train, with tonnage adjusted accordingly. A 2-6-6-6 is on the head end. Date: June 1947, Place: Avis Yard, east end of Hinton.

Gene Huddleston

A C&O westbound empty hopper train runs swiftly along the wide New River at Brooks, West Virginia, in 1945 headed by an H-8 2-6-6-6 locomotive. The series of low falls in the river at this point is caused by the Hinton Sandstone dipping below the bed of the river.

C&O Ry; C&O Historical Society Collection

16

Behind the C&0 2-8-8-2, making its double before leaving Avis yard at Hinton, is the confluence of the New and Greenbrier. The Greenbrier will take the C&O's Alleghany Subdivision beyond the Alleghany Front to the edge of the Ridge and Valley Province. Glen Lyn, Virginia, 26 miles up the New from this point, was where both the Virginian and N&W descended from the plateau to river level. The big "Simon" built by Alco in 1924 was 19 years old when this wartime photo was taken.

The Alleghany Front

The "Alleghany Front" is the name given the eastern escarpment of the Appalachian Plateau Province. A "border land" lies between the plateau and the first great ridge of the Valley and Ridge Province. This "border" country is largely a low, limestone plateau.

An eastbound coal train approaches Alderson, West Virginia, in May 1980. The ridge line in the background is the Alleghany Front, the eastern escarpment of the Alleghany Plateau. Behind this ridge are jumbled hills, and ahead of the train are the high ridges of the Ridge and Valley Province. The prominence on the ridge above the locomotives is Keeney's Knob, a Monadnock .

Amid the shadows of late afternoon on a winter's day in 1971, manifest No. 95, headed by five units, speeds west downgrade at Alderson, West Virginia, in the "border land" between the Appalachian Plateau and Ridge and Valley Province. The five units were needed for climbing to the summit of the Alleghanies at Alleghany, Virginia, about 30 miles behind the train.

Thomas W. Dixon, Jr.

Gary E. Huddleston

The largely undisturbed horizontal bedding of the rocks behind this four-unit eastbound coal train in May 1957 is evidence that the train is still within the Appalachian Plateau. Fort Spring Tunnel was constructed in 1946-47 as part of Robert R. Young's line-straightening campaign. It eliminated a long curve caused by a sharp bend in the Greenbrier River, which the railroad follows from Hinton to the base of the "folded" Alleghanies beyond Ronceverte.

C&O Ry; C&O Historical Society Collection

This earlier photo shows the same scene but at the opposite (west) portal with the first train out of the new tunnel in November 1947, a local freight led by K-3 class Mikado No. 1229. Note that one track is still unballasted.

The Valley and Ridge Province

C&O enters this province as soon as its mainline crosses the Greenbrier River east of Ronceverte, West Virginia.

Gene Huddleston; Herbert H. Harwood, Jr. Collection

In June 1951, Berkshire 2764 proves its mettle as a passenger engine in rapidly accelerating *The Sportsman* up the 0.56 percent grade east of White Sulphur Springs station. A westbound behind H-8 No. 1626 at right makes for a dramatic meet. This action takes place on the Alleghany Subdivision, 80 miles of mountain territory located mostly in the Valley and Ridge Province.

Three trains in one photo! A train of empty coal cars, headed by a 2-6-6-6 (out of sight) is stopped at the White Sulphur Springs depot (behind the photographer), awaiting arrival of local No. 13, headed by the 2-8-4 shown here in the foreground. In the siding is a 2-6-6-2 on the local freight eastbound in 1951.

Gene Huddleston

East of White Sulphur Springs in a valley between two great ridges of the Alleghanies, a 2-6-6-6 runs downgrade on its return "light" to Hinton after shoving an eastbound coal train to the summit at Alleghany, Virginia, in June 1951.

Gene Huddleston

In 1951 less than two miles east of White Sulphur Springs, Alleghany type 1624 shoves an eastbound coal train up the valley of Dry Creek, which trends in a southwesterly direction in conformity with the general trend of the Valley and Ridge Province. At top of ridge in right background is the Virginia-West Virginia state line.

Gene Huddleston

20

The Alleghany Subdivision local freight heads east two miles east of White Sulphur Springs along the valley of Dry Creek. Thick layer of cinders from locomotive exhausts coat the right-of-way.

Gene Huddleston

Twin EMD E8 "A" units, equipped with air-cooling radiators on the roof, bring No. 46, *The Sportsman*, around the long curve at Tuckahoe, West Virginia, about 7:30 am in December 1957. The train will soon tunnel under the ridge at right. Slide detector fence, rising above last four cars, protects right-of-way from shale bedded at a 45 degree angle.

Gary E. Huddleston

Two manifests, both powered by 2-6-6-6s, meet a quarter mile east of Alleghany depot in June 1947. The tunnel under the ridge marking the boundary between West Virginia and Virginia (and the Atlantic-Gulf watershed) is about a half mile beyond the curve to the left.

C&O Historical Society Collection; by Gene Huddleston

21

C&O passenger local No. 13 in May 1957 emerges from Lewis Tunnel in the "folded" Alleghanies. (The pitch of the alternating layers of sandstone and shale in the background is roughly 45 degrees.) At Alleghany, Virginia, which No. 13 approaches, were two mainline tracks and two passing sidings.

Westbound empties in 1957 climb the 1.14 percent grade to the summit of the ridge marking the Atlantic-Gulf watershed at Alleghany, Virginia. Here, just east of Jerry's Run, Virginia , the train has climbed far above Dunlap Creek in the valley below. The long "parallel" ridge in the background is Peters Mountain, essentially the same ridge that the New River cuts through at Narrows, Virginia (to the southwest), along the Virginian and N&W lines.

In 1952 westbound H-8 No. 1635 works easily over the Alleghany Subdivision near Covington, Virginia. The 1.14 percent grade to the summit begins west of town. Behind is one of the long, parallel ridges marking the Valley and Ridge Province.

A first-rate illustration of a true "folded" mountain! Behind this Mike, with the local freight off the James River Subdivision, is a vivid illustration of the "folding" of rocks which produced the parallel ridges of the Ridge and Valley Province. Known as "Rainbow Rock" this Silurion anticline was exposed when the Jackson River cut a gap through it. Here at the east end of the Clifton Forge yard, is the junction of the Mountain Subdivision and James River line.

C&O Ry; C&O Historical Society Collection

Another view of Rainbow Rock, this time looking east as a C&O freight moves along the James River Subdivision trackage between Iron Gate and Clifton Forge yard in 1946.

C&O Ry; C&O Historical Society Collection

Eagle Mountain, (or Eagle Rock) Virginia, is where the James River cuts through the last great ridge of the Valley and Ridge Province near the province's eastern boundary. This is the mountain showing behind 4-8-4 No. 614 stopped on the mainline, awaiting a meet with the westbound James River local freight in August 1952. North of here the ridge is known as Great North Mountain. The Hancock feedwater heater used on the 5 J-3A C&0 4-8-4s was a rarity. It was missing when 614 was later restored to service.

Gene Huddleston

The Great Valley

This historical valley (recall Stonewall Jackson's Valley Campaign) extends from one end of Virginia to the other and separates the Alleghanies (the Valley and Ridge Province) from the much older mass of the Blue Ridge.

Robert F. Collins

At Balcony Falls the Great Valley is flat and at its narrowest in Virginia. This view, looking east, shows the looming mass of the Blue Ridge forming the boundary of the Valley. Behind the ballast cars, hauled by K-3 Mike 1257 in May 1951, is the junction of the branch which heads up the valley to Lexington. Behind the photographer is the Balcony Falls depot and coal dock.

Jeremy Taylor; C&O Historical Society Collection

A Pere Marquette Railway Berkshire, No. 1218, brings an empty train of 98 cars west at Buchanan, Virginia, as reflected in the still waters of the James River in September 1952. The Pere Marquette locomotives were moved to the old C&O when the PM lines were dieselized in the late 1940s and early 1950s (the C&O had absorbed the PM in 1947).

The Blue Ridge

"In the Blue Ridge Mountains of Virginia, on the Trail of the Lonesome Pine." This and many songs have been composed about these scenic mountains, known as the Catoctin in Maryland and Smokies in North Carolina.

C&O had no Blue Ridge grade for its coal trains, for the railroad used the gap cut in the mountain chain by the James River. This view, taken from the rear of a train in 1957, shows the rapid river and three-mile gorge created by the passage. Few if any other photos have been taken in this area between Balcony Falls and Snowden, which is quite difficult of access.

J. Randolph Kean

The passage of the James River through the Blue Ridge, like most water gaps, is a scene to be marveled at.

Virginia: A Guide to the Old Dominion provides an informative entry for Balcony Falls: "a series of rapids in the beautiful gap, cut by the James through the Blue Ridge. Because the James and the Potomac are the only streams offering possibilities of water transportation between Chesapeake Bay and the valleys beyond the range, plans were made for their utilization as early as 1772. Although the first section of the James River Canal was opened in 1789, more than 50 years had passed and $8,000,000 had been spent before the canal was carried beyond Balcony Falls. However, sluice navigation was being used by 1816. Long narrow bateaux loaded with produce were guided through the tortuous channel by boatmen whose services drew high pay. The railroad through this pass was completed in 1881."

East of Big Island, Virginia, the James River local freight heads down the James River in August 1961. About seven miles back is the main mass of the Blue Ridge, through which the river cuts a gap near Balcony Falls.

Gene Huddleston

THE MOUNTAIN SUBDIVISION

At Clifton Forge, Virginia, the C&O's main line to the east branches in two separate directions: one down the James River to Newport News and Norfolk and the other literally over the Valley and Ridge Province to Washington, D.C. The former line is identified as the James River Subdivision; the latter as the Mountain. Both cross the same physiographic sections: Valley and Ridge, Great Valley, and Blue Ridge.

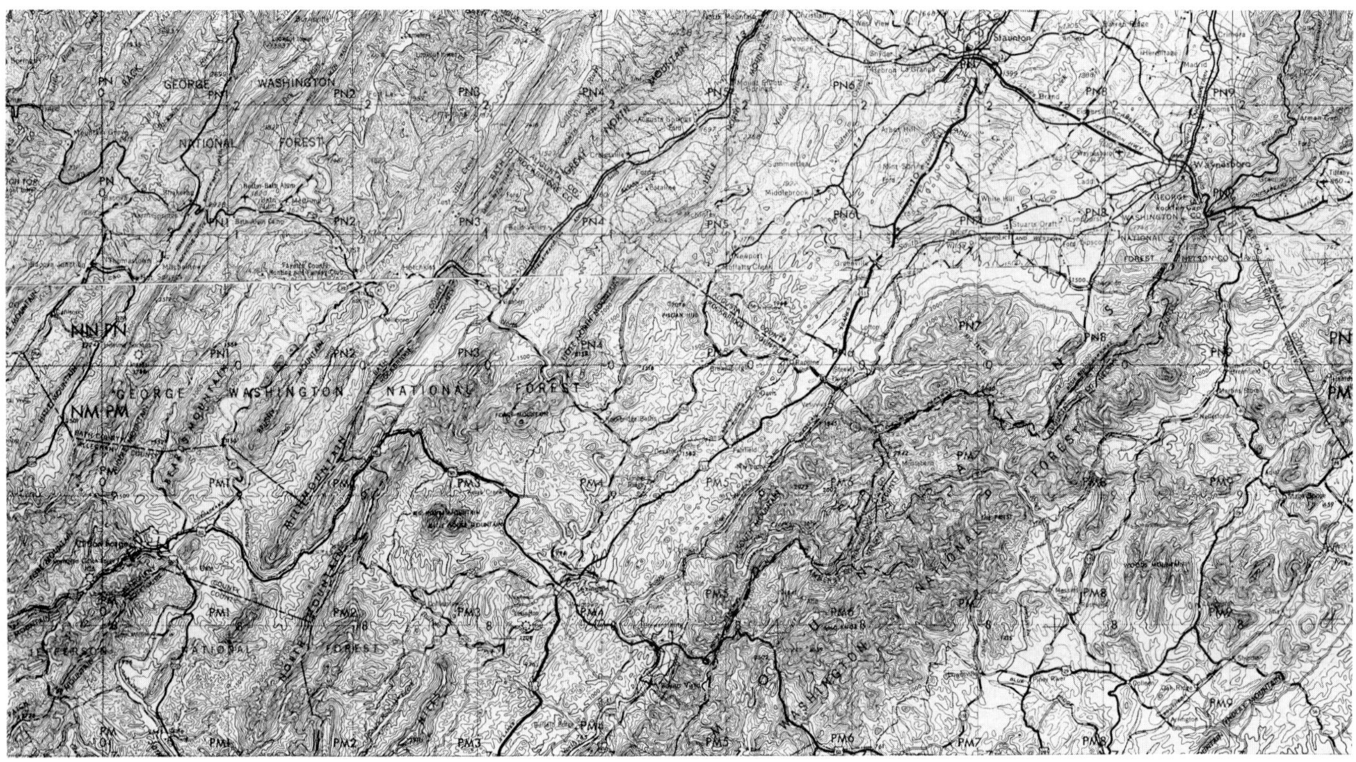

The main focus of map "B" is C&O's scenic Mountain Subdivision over which *The George Washington* ran and the Amtrak *Cardinal* still does (though not for long). Note how the tracks follow valleys between ridges in the Valley and Ridge Province. Out of Clifton Forge the single-track line keeps between Brushy Mountain and Mill Mountain, finally cutting directly east into another major valley at Panther Gap (the Gap in Mill Mountain between *Millboro* and *Goshen*). From Goshen the tracks run between Great North Mountain and Little North Mountain. Then at *North Mountain* station the tracks cut through Buffalo Gap and descend into the Great Valley. (*Staunton* is in the middle of the Valley.) Just east of *Waynesboro* the tracks ascend the Blue Ridge to Blue Ridge Tunnel, at Rockfish Gap, and then gradually descend the east slope to the Piedmont Region at Charlottesville (out of picture). Elliott Knob, a prominent Monadnock of Great North Mountain, is off the map just north of North Mountain station.

No. 5, *The Sportsman*, out of Washington, ascends Longdale Hill in August 1948 with Steam-turbine-electric locomotive No. 500 for power. Three of these monster experimental locomotives were built for use on *The Chessie*, but were diverted to other trains when *The Chessie* was cancelled. The 500s were ultimately to be scrapped after only a year of service—a great failure. This steep, short hill takes the tracks over a minor divide between the Cow Pasture River and the Jackson River. About a year or two before this photo was taken, this section of the Mountain Subdivision had been relocated to reduce curvature and lower the summit somewhat.

Gene Huddleston

The Valley and Ridge and Great Valley both appear in this panoramic view near Staunton, Virginia. Near Snyder, Virginia, a C&O Geep brings the Mountain Subdivision local freight across the Great Valley of Virginia in September 1958. Against the horizon is Elliott Knob, over 4,200 feet in elevation, which rises as a Monadnock in this section of the Valley and Ridge Province. Elliott Knob is part of the long ridge known as Great North Mountain, in front of which is Little North Mountain. In between is Buffalo Gap, through which the local freight passed some nine miles back.

Gene Huddleston

C&O's Mountain Subdivision crosses the Blue Ridge two miles east of Waynesboro. A C&O westbound manifest over the Mountain Subdivision leaves the passing siding at Waynesboro, in 1969, after an eastbound passenger has just cleared. The freight has just crossed the Blue Ridge, the main mass of which is in the background. It will now cross the Great Valley (or Shenandoah) before ascending North Mountain in the Ridge and Valley Province.

William E. Warden, Jr.

The summit of the Blue Ridge
grade is at about the spot where
J-3a Greenbrier No. 614 exits the
"new" 1944 Blue Ridge Tunnel
in 1948. (The West portal of the
original tunnel is slightly behind
the photographer and to the left.)

J. I. Kelly Collection; C&O Historical Society

In September 1961, the C&O's
Sportsman starts descending the
east slope of the Blue Ridge at
Afton station. The white building
at top of photo stands at Rockfish
Gap. Blue Ridge Tunnel, nearly a
mile long, takes the railroad under
the Gap.

Gene Huddleston

This passenger train is descending
the east slope of the Blue Ridge, but
one doesn't get the "larger picture"
because of the rather confined area
embraced by the photo. *The Sportsman*, headed by steam-turbine-electric No. 501, is at the east end of the
passing siding at Greenwood, Virginia, July 13, 1948.

J. I. Kelly; D. Wallace Johnson Collection

Chapter II

The Norfolk and Western Railway

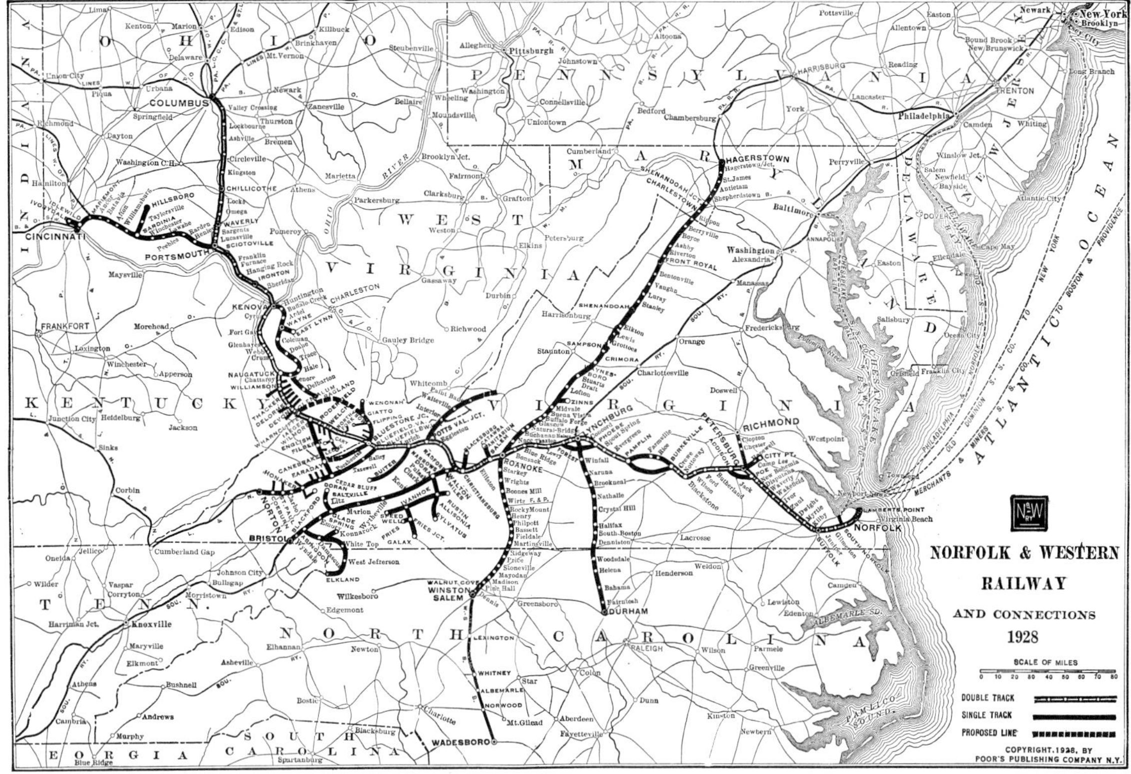

The N&W System as it appeared about 1928 (from *Poor's Manual of the Railroads*).

The Appalachian Plateau

Gene Huddleston

Gene Huddleston

This class J (4-8-4), awaiting the signal to depart Ironton, Ohio, is hauling *The Cavalier* west down the broad valley of the Ohio River, bordered on both sides by the hills of the Appalachian Plateau. Ironton, built on a low flood plain of the Ohio is protected by a flood wall (at right) constructed after the 1937 flood sent water to a height of about eight feet at this point in the city.

The Powhatan Arrow leaves Ironton, Ohio, in 1953. Its next stop will be Kenova, West Virginia, and then Prichard, to take coal and water. Before dark N&W train No. 26 will have traversed, via many twists and turns, the most scenic vistas of the Tug Valley coal country.

Gene Huddleston

Gene Huddleston

Along the riverfront through Ironton, a class J accelerates the five-car streamliner, *The Powhatan Arrow* , eastward past a 2-6-6-2 on a work train in 1953.

In May 1957 the westbound *Cavalier* pauses at Fort Gay, West Virginia, on the banks of the Big Sandy River (to right of photo). The hills in the background are part of the Appalachian Plateau. They are lower in this western part of the state because the Plateau gradually slopes upward as it trends in a southeasterly direction.

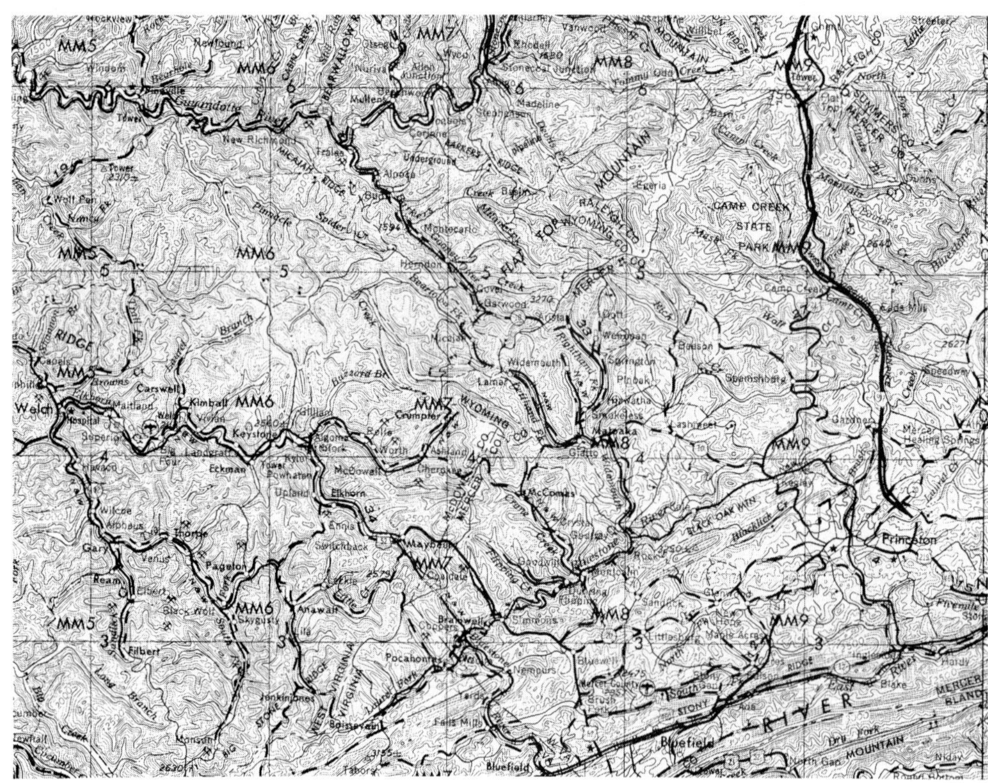

The focus of Map "C", which covers mostly the Appalachian Plateau, is the climb to the summit of Great Flat Top Mountain by both the Virginian and the Norfolk and Western. The N&W climb, which begins at *Welch*, parallels U.S. 52 to *Maybeury*. Elkhorn Tunnel is clearly visible at *Coaldale*. The Virginian climb up to the top of the Plateau begins at Elmore yards, *Mullens* (which stretches along the Guyandotte between Mullens and *Tralee*) and ends at the summit tunnel near *Lamar* (Clarks Gap). The Alleghany Front escarpment is marked by Stony Ridge (bottom right corner of map), which closely adjoins the westernmost ridge of the Valley and Ridge Province; namely, East River Mountain, identified easily by noting the state line dividing Mercer County, West Virginia from Bland County, Virginia. Coal deposits are found roughly west of a line drawn from *Falls Mills* (bottom center) to *Josephine* (top).

The passengers on the eastbound Powhatan Arrow can enjoy from their windows the pastel greens of the April hillsides and wonder at the infinitely varied ridge line on the horizon across the Tug Fork. (The train, near Kermit, West Virginia, in 1957, is just across the river from Kentucky).

Gene Huddleston

In Appalachia (i.e., the Appalachian Plateau) almost every valley and "hollow" in coal country once had a railroad branch line running through it. Here, in April 1957, on the Lenore branch a short distance up Dingess Run, near Williamson, West Virginia, N&W mountain-type No. 103 waits while an operating problem is cleared up.

Gene Huddleston

In December 1958 the engineer of a 190-car train of empty coal cars powered by EMD diesels is about to pick up orders at Kermit, West Virginia, in the valley of the Tug Fork. The crew on the 2-8-8-2 in the background, taking lunch, will head out of the siding as soon as the mainline train clears, and will move up the valley to pull loads at coal mines near Warfield, Kentucky.

Gary E. Huddleston

Y-6a 2166 pulls out onto the main at Kermit soon after diesel Extra 621 has cleared in December 1958.

Gary E. Huddleston

Through a West Virginia coal camp near Naugatuck on the Tug Fork, a 190-car coal train, headed by class A 1209, works at full throttle through the many twists and turns of the crooked river on its way via the Tug, Big Sandy and Ohio to Portsmouth, Ohio, in April 1957. Rivers and other streams provide the only feasible rail routes into and out of the Appalachian Plateau.

Gene Huddleston

A class A, fully loaded with 30 tons of coal and about 45,000 gallons of water (including auxiliary tank), has pulled up to the west end of the yards at Williamson in 1953 preparatory to coupling onto a 175-car coal train which it will take down the Tug, Big Sandy and Ohio to Portsmouth without stopping for either coal or water.

Gene Huddleston

The eastbound *Powhatan Arrow* blasts away from the station at Williamson, West Virginia, in 1953 as class A No. 1211 (2-6-6-4) prepares to couple onto 175 coal cars (the head end showing behind the 4-8-4) for the trip west to Portsmouth, Ohio, following first the Tug Fork, then Big Sandy, and finally "the beautiful Ohio". The class J will parallel the Tug Fork and then Elkhorn Creek to climb to the top of the Alleghany Plateau.

Gene Huddleston

A westbound coal train heads down Tug Fork just around the bend from Matewan, West Virginia, a coal mining town that was the subject of the John Sayles 1986 film of the same title. Bridge in background takes N&W branch into Pike County, Kentucky.

N&W; VPI&SU Archives

Auville yard at Iaeger, West Virginia, is at the confluence of Dry Creek with Tug Fork. In later steam days 2-8-8-2s and 2-6-6-2s stationed here supplied the many large coal mines in the area.

Gene Huddleston

Gene Huddleston

Two 2-8-8-2s await service at Auville yard, Iaeger. The steep hills of the Appalachian Plateau provide a cozy setting for the little engine terminal. The angle of this 1959 photo offers a good view of the large compensating lever for the front-end throttle of 2105 (the reach-rod for which can be seen entering the steam dome just behind the stack atop the boiler).

In September 1957 a Y6b shoves a long coal train along the banks of the Tug Fork near Roderfield, West Virginia, between Iaeger and Welch. The caboose is coupled behind the auxiliary tender. At Farm, near Welch, the tonnage will be cut down for the climb up Elkhorn Creek to Elkhorn Tunnel under Flat Top Mountain. The 2-8-8-2s powered practically all freights over the mountainous Pocahontas Division.

Gene Huddleston

In later years N&W "standardized" its motive power with four modern types: the S-1 0-8-0 switcher (of C&O origin); the class J 4-8-4; class A 2-6-6-4; and Y-6 2-8-8-2. Although of different design, they shared (1) high capacity boiler with large grate area; (2) one-piece cast-steel bed frames with cylinders cast integral; (3) roller bearings on all axles; and (4) complete mechanical and pressure lubrication.

D. Wallace Johnson

A very rare photo (1954) of coaling station at Farm, West Virginia. Although only 1.6 miles west of Welch, seat of McDowell County on the Tug Fork, the place was difficult of access, with a winding single lane dirt road the only way in. Note sand spout descending from cylindrical tower at top of structure. The four tracks here include the two mainline tracks and two set-off tracks for reducing tonnage for the climb ahead.

THE ELKHORN GRADE

The following series of photos, made in the heart of Appalachia, date from June 1959 and cover in sequence the passage of a coal train out of a deep valley in the Appalachian Plateau to the top of the Plateau. The Elkhorn grade begins at the confluence of Elkhorn Creek with the Tug Fork of the Big Sandy near Welch and continues for about 18 miles to near the head of this creek before tunneling under Great Flat Top Mountain, a Monadnock rising above the general level of the Plateau, which itself slopes steadily upward in a southeasterly direction. The grade, then, is long and steep, being 1.4 percent for nine miles near its top. The tunnel which existed at the time of the photos had been built in 1950 and was the longest on N&W's main line. (A shorter tunnel at a higher altitude, single-tracked and with restrictive clearances, could not be ventilated properly, thus early necessitating electrification of this line until the new tunnel was built.) Between Kimball, near the bottom of the grade, and the west portal of Elkhorn Tunnel was the most exciting steam action on the Norfolk and Western—more spectacular than either its Blue Ridge or the Alleghany grades, because loaded coal trains ascended the Elkhorn.

Accompanying this series is a letter from an engineer on N&W's Pocahontas Division who handled Y-6b No.'2183 that June morning on the chase along U.S. 52. The engineer, constantly aware of two young men in a '57 Olds photographing his train, decided he would like some of the photos, so he wrote a note, attached it with a rubber band to a piece of coal, and threw it off as his engine crossed the bridge over U.S. 52 at the last point on the chase where the train could be photographed before it entered Elkhorn Tunnel. I was shooting Kodachrome with a Sears imitation Leica (with Nikkor Lens), and my brother Gary was using a 4x5 press camera. So we sent him with our (and H. W. Pontin's) compliments a set of photos. In reply we received this answer to our queries about his trip that heavily overcast June morning: "I received those wonderful pictures today of the steam engines. Although they are very dirty and much more work than diesels, they seem to talk to you when the pressure is really put on them. . . . I will try to answer the questions for you the best I can.

"On June 13 I was called in Williamson at 3:15 AM and was relieved in Bluefield at 10:15 AM; it is some one hundred four miles. There are four curves which have a twenty mph restriction on them and we had 165 cars, between 14,000 and 15,000 tons that morning. The diesel pusher reported in Williamson also as it is upgrade all the way, and you get all the speed you can get without getting caught on restricted curves.

35

"The new Elkhorn Tunnel is very nice; there are two huge fans on the west end of the tunnel, one on each side which keeps the smoke ahead of   you. The old tunnel—well, let's say just 'Grin and bear it'. We carried overall jackets which we covered our heads with and ran an air hose up under it which helped; later they put fans on some of the engines, but no one used them because the fan picked up cinders and threw them in your face.

"Yes, there are some steam at Iaeger, Williamson, and Weller yard, which is eight miles from Grundy. They are used at Iaeger and Weller yard on mine runs and pushers and from Williamson to Weller yard and Williamson to Gilbert (Virginian connection) sometimes. Weller yard would be a good place as they have a grade about seven miles up one side and seven miles down the other side. They will have steam at least until some time in January and they really thrash them. No, steam power is through east of Iaeger with the exception of shifters going from Iaeger to the Wilcoe branch. There isn't much going on now due to the steel strike, though we haven't been hit so hard in this field. I think they have been loading on the average of 15 to 17,000 cars per week.

"Well, I suppose that run was about the best run I have ever made because we reduced tonnage at Farm (just west of Welch) for Elkhorn Mt. that morning. I think we had 87 cars or about 7700 tons. They had cut out the coal wharf at Farm but were to have a man there to give me coal, sand, and water, so I think he gave me an extra show, and I took advantage of it.

"Well, I want to thank you again for the pictures; my three kids got a real thrill out of them. After I told them the story, Randy, my boy, says dat's my daddy's engine. Thanks again and good shooting on your next trip; tell your brother hello and be careful. Hope to see you both taking pictures again soon. I think I would know you now.

Yours very truly, S. R. Scott, Jr."

Stoker works at full capacity (note its exhaust under cab) as extra 2183, east of Welch, near Maitland, starts up the Elkhorn grade. It had received its own Alco diesel pushers at Farm, west of Welch. The pushers shown are waiting for the next train east to be pulled by Y-6b No. 2199. Near this point the mainline leaves the Tug Fork to start climbing to the source of its tributary, Elkhorn Creek.

Gary E. Huddleston

About to enter one of the twin tunnels near Kimball, engineer Scott is working a full throttle but has not as yet opened the "booster valve." Fireman has crossed gangway to see photographers that engineer has told him about.

Gary E. Huddleston

Y-6b 2183 never slipped once going up Elkhorn Mountain! Even with the booster valve on, the heavy lead weights that had been added to cavities in the casting of the front frame provided the needed adhesion for the drivers.

The engineer on 2183 has just turned on the "booster" valve, for the eastbound train is now at Eckman, on "Elkhorn Mountain" and approaching the steepest part of the grade. During electrification (until 1950) Eckman was an engine terminal, where steamers were exchanged for electrics for the climb to the old summit tunnel at Coaldale.

Gary E. Huddleston

Gary E. Huddleston

Grinding sand beneath its wheels, 2183 gradually lifts its tonnage through Keystone, West Virginia, toward the summit of Flat Top Mountain. Built in 1949, 2183 had a boiler pressure of 300 pounds, 58 inch drivers, 106 square feet of grate area, and 127,000 pounds of tractive effort, working in compound. With a BL-2 feedwater heater and an American multiple front-end throttle, it was modern in every respect.

You'd better believe the "booster" in the cab has been turned on; there's no other way to account for the uninterrupted and voluminous cascade of smoke and steam that mark the passage of Extra 2183 East through North Fork, West Virginia. The "booster", controlled by a globe valve, is not the same as the simpling device, controlled by an angle valve in the cab. The "booster" feeds a comparatively small amount of superheated, high pressure steam into the "used" (low pressure) steam heading to the front cylinders from the rear. This boost in steam pressure raises considerably the drawbar horsepower of the 2-8-8-2 on an upgrade pull. The simpling valve was used to increase starting tractive effort by sending high pressure steam directly to both sets of cylinders. (Thus the rear set of cylinders exhausted into a pipe bypassing the front cylinders.) Operating in simple consumed so much steam that, unlike the booster valve, it could not be long sustained in operation. Although simpling was common on all Mallet compounds, the application of a booster burst of steam to front cylinders to increase power at speed was worked out solely by the N&W.

Gary E. Huddleston

North Fork, 10 miles east of Maitland and about six miles from Elkhorn Tunnel, is at the junction of North Fork and main Elkhorn Creek. Before the advent of roads through the narrow valley, one traveled by railroad, or if he had a buggy or "tin lizzie" he used the bed of the creek as a road. The 2183 is exerting maximum drawbar horsepower as engineer Scott takes eastbound coal over N&W's most interesting division — the Pocahontas.

Gene Huddleston

The distinctive front end of the N&W's big 2-8-8-2s was produced by large low pressure cylinders coupled with extra large piston valves and huge exhaust pipes aimed at a 45-degree angle upward to decrease deflection of the jet-like force of the exhaust, a design necessary to reduce "back pressure" in the cylinders.

If the exhaust from 2183 looks like it's being thrown up at a slightly forward angle, it is. The exhaust stand, petticoat pipe, and stack are set to throw the exhaust 5 degrees forward off the vertical. The engineer has left his seat box to find a piece of coal to weigh down a message to throw off. Coal supply in tender has disappeared from sight, even though 2183 took on a full supply at Farm, about 15 miles back.

Gary E. Huddleston

The old line continued up the hollow behind the locomotive before tunneling through Flat Top Mountain. Here at Maybeury, 2183 crosses a new bridge over the creek and over U.S. 52, comprising a lower approach to the mountain and requiring a much longer tunnel. Engineer Scott is about ready to throw off his note, an act which luckily photographer Gary Huddleston observed.

Gary E. Huddleston

Extra 2199 East ran just a few minutes behind Extra 2183 East This photo was made about a half mile from the new Elkhorn Tunnel. Speed, is down now to about 12 miles per hour. A slide-detector fence is behind the locomotive. No tracks had been in this area before 1950.

Gary E. Huddleston

Gary E. Huddleston

Big blowers at Elkhorn Tunnel are about to go on as 2199, assisted by three Alco road switchers on the rear, nears the top of the Appalachian Plateau. The near 7,000-foot bore penetrates Flat Top Mountain, which forms the Alleghany Front at the eastern edge of the Appalachian Plateau. The name Elkhorn derives from Elkhorn Creek which the train has been ascending since leaving Welch. The grade is steep, for at Welch the altitude above sea level is 1,297 feet and here at the tunnel, 22 miles away, it is 2,380 feet. The old tunnel, which this one replaced, is about a half-mile from here; its narrow clearances made for pure hell for the crews until the line was electrified. The contractor for the old tunnel made extra money because it was drilled mostly through thick coal seam Pocahontas No. 3, the second most important seam in the history of West Virginia mining (the first in importance being the Pittsburgh seam). Top of the slide detector fence shows over the top of the coal cars. The fence protects against slides from sandstones and shales in the cut.

Valley and Ridge

N&W; VPI&SU Archives

In 1960 new N&W GP9s and GP18s westbound follow the New River as it cuts through the heart of the Valley and Ridge Province about two miles west of Narrows, Virginia. This view captures the Narrows itself, with Peters Mountain on the left and its extension, East River Mountain, on the right. The ridge barely showing through the haze is Angel's Rest. Scarring the slope of Peters Mountain is "Devil's Slide." The Virginian mainline is across the river, a section abandoned because of highway relocation more than 10 years after the 1959 N&W merger.

40

An eastbound coal train blasts up the New River through the Narrows just west of Narrows, Virginia. In the foreground is the electric catenary of the Virginian Railway. In the back is Angel's Rest. The rapids in the river are formed by the resistant, upturned layer of rock forming the "Devil's Slide" on Peter's Mountain (at left).

N&W; VPI&SU Archives

The New River from Glen Lyn to Radford, Virginia, was unmatched for combining beautiful scenery with heavy traffic. On the east bank of the river was the single-track electrified Virginian. On the west bank, the double-track N&W. And both were main lines.

Behind excursion locomotive No. 611, headed east, or up river, in 1982, is Peters Mountain at the Narrows of New River. The vein of highly resistant sandstone slicing at an angle up the side of the mountain is locally called the "Devil's Slide" and forms the backbone of the long ridge called Peters Mountain at right and East River Mountain (out of sight to left).

Ron Piskor

The small town of Narrows, Virginia, has a lovely setting between two great parallel ridges, trending southwest to the northeast. At the highest point on this ridge overlooking New River Valley, aptly named Angel's Rest, the altitude is 3,633 feet above sea level. Behind the photographer is the northernmost parallel ridge, called East River Mountain to the east of the New with Peters Mountain to the west. The train shown is eastbound in April 1986.

Gene Huddleston

In another perspective of Angel's Rest Mountain and the N&W main line, one sees the depot at Narrows, April 1986. (The actual narrows in the New River is behind the photographer about two miles where the river cuts through the high ridge forming East River Mountain and Peters Mountain.

Gene Huddleston

Over former Virginian trackage on the east bank of the New near Pembroke, a Norfolk Southern coal train, powered by two General Electric C39-8 units, heads for Roanoke in the mid 1980s. A close look at the limestone (dolomite) cliffs shows their tendency to weather and fracture into spires. To obtain photos of train and palisades together, the Norfolk Southern photographer resorted to a helicopter.

Norfolk Southern

N&W; Roanoke Chapter NRHS

2-8-8-2 No. 2141 heads up the New River in the Valley and Ridge Province west (north) of Pembroke around 1940. (The train has stopped for the photographer in a largely inaccessible location.) In background is brow of Angel's Rest Mountain. The river, in cutting across the Province, has entrenched itself some 400 feet below the "Valley" level into thick beds of limestone and dolomite that weather into vertical columns, or spires.

In April 1986, a westbound manifest runs down the New River near Pembroke over the former Virginian electrified trackage. Across the river are limestone and dolomite palisades forming a bluff by-passed , by N&W's 299-foot Pembroke Tunnel. Note unusual rock spire at left. (For a photo taken almost directly across river, see Richard Cook's dramatic action photo of 2173, emerging from tunnel on next page.)

Gene Huddleston

Richard J. Cook

Slide-detector fences protect the tracks and "tell tails" (no longer used) protect employees standing on top of equipment, as Extra 2173 East blasts up New River in June 1956, across from Pembroke. Huge cliffs of limestone and dolomite line both sides of the river between Eggleston and Norcross. Behind the Y-6b is Pembroke Tunnel, 299 feet long.

Over former Virginian Railway trackage on the east bank of the New River, Class J No. 611 (4-8-4) handles an excursion of 22 cars, sponsored by the Roanoke Chapter of the National Railway Historical Society in 1982. The eastbound train is passing under the Pinnacles (or Palisades) of the New at Eggleston, a series of spires composed of limestone and dolomite.

It's early evening by the time eastbound daylight streamliner *The Powhatan Arrow* reaches Belspring, Virginia, on the New River late in 1946. The high ridge in the distance is Big Walker Mountain, the last major mountain ridge seen from the train before it leaves the Ridge and Valley Province.

The Great Valley

N&W; VPI&SU Archives

An eastbound manifest train near Elliston, Virginia, descends Christiansburg Mountain into the Great Valley.

The Blue Ridge

Herbert H. Harwood, Jr.

Three engines are required to lift this 12,800-ton coal train east up Blue Ridge. In the five miles from Bonsack to Blue Ridge, the grade has short segments ranging from level to 1.34 percent but the ruling grade is 1.2 percent, for it is sustained the longest distance, about a mile. Class A 1242 is assisted by two Y-6 2-8-8-2s, one on front and the other on the rear. Both will uncouple at the summit and return to Roanoke. Here, on the last three miles of the pull, speed is down to below 10 miles per hour and the two Mallet compounds are working in the "simple" mode in June 1958.

The focus of map "D" is the Blue Ridge crossing of the Norfolk & Western. Highway US 460 parallels the old N&W grade all the way from Roanoke to Bedford, so that fact coupled with the high traffic volume made this area popular with railfan photographers. The summit of the Blue Ridge range is indicated by the line dividing Botetourt County from Bedford County (and by the Blue Ridge Parkway). The "pass" in the Blue Ridge that the N&W follows is clearly indicated by the contour lines. These same lines indicate that the narrowest part of the gap (called Buford's Gap) is at Villamont, two miles east of Blue Ridge station. The twin Peaks of Otter, the most prominent physical feature in the area, are west of Peaksville (north of Bedford). The map covers mostly the Great Valley, Blue Ridge, and Piedmont Province. Also on the map (at top) are two portions of C&O's winding James River line; the passage of this line through the Blue Ridge is off the map at top. At bottom left the Virginian Railway leaves Roanoke via the Roanoke River but then cuts overland to head down a tributary of the Roanoke, Goose Creek.

Compound Y6 Mallet No. 2131 (2-8-8-2) nears the summit eastbound on the steepest part of the west slope of Blue Ridge. The 2131's train is on about three-quarters of a mile of 1.20 percent that constitutes the ruling grade eastbound. Steam still dominates on Blue Ridge in June 1957!

Thomas J. Donahue

In June 1958, Class A 1236 (2-6-6-4) one-half mile west of Blue Ridge station is fighting a 1.2 percent grade to the summit. Surprisingly, there are no tunnels on this grade, even at the top, which is relatively level, topographically.

Herbert H. Harwood, Jr.

Herbert H. Harwood, Jr.

No. 1236 tops the Blue Ridge summit just east of Blue Ridge station about 11 miles east of Roanoke, at a sag in the range known as Buford's Gap. The class A 2-6-6-4 eastbound is just topping a mile or so of 1.2 percent grade. Reverse gear is "in the corner" for the uphill pull.

Herbert H. Harwood, Jr.

Only the front end of class A No. 1236 East shows as it slowly surmounts the summit at Blue Ridge depot. But class A 1231, with a westbound manifest, is moving considerably faster, having most of its train over the top of the grade, located about a half mile east of the depot in March 1958.

John Krause; T. W. Dixon, Jr. Collection

An eastbound local headed by 4-8-4 No. 606 drops down the short but steep grade leading from the summit of the Blue Ridge between Blue Ridge Station and Montvale. The N&W main line makes use of a "wind gap" for a fairly easy passage over the summit of the Blue Ridge, some 11 miles east of Roanoke.

Simple articulated class A No. 1230 magnificently lifts a west-bound manifest up the Blue Ridge grade at Villamont, one mile short of the summit. Its train is on the near one mile of 1.35 percent which constitutes the steepest grade on either side of the hill. In the background of this June 1957 scene are the Peaks of Otter.

Thomas J. Donahue

Herbert H. Harwood, Jr.

The 1236, in March 1958, passes through Buford Gap in the Blue Ridge as it brings 190 empty coal cars back from Tidewater to the coal fields. Pusher engines taking siding keep the rails of the center siding shining.

Herbert H. Harwood, Jr.

The photographer chased class A 1221 west through the Piedmont in March 1958. The Blue Ridge Mountains loom to the left out of the picture.

Herbert H. Harwood, Jr.

This class A 1221 with auxiliary water tender is not working to capacity as it slows in obeying a restrictive signal on its way westward near the bottom of the Blue Ridge grade in March 1958.

N&W; VPI&SU Archives

The angularities of the twin Peaks of Otter, northwest of Bedford, remind one of the Rockies more than the Blue Ridge. They dominate the landscape for many miles.

Herbert H. Harwood, Jr.

In March 1958 Extra 1221 West is approaching the Blue Ridge range. But here, near Bedford, the train is actually in the Piedmont physiographic province.

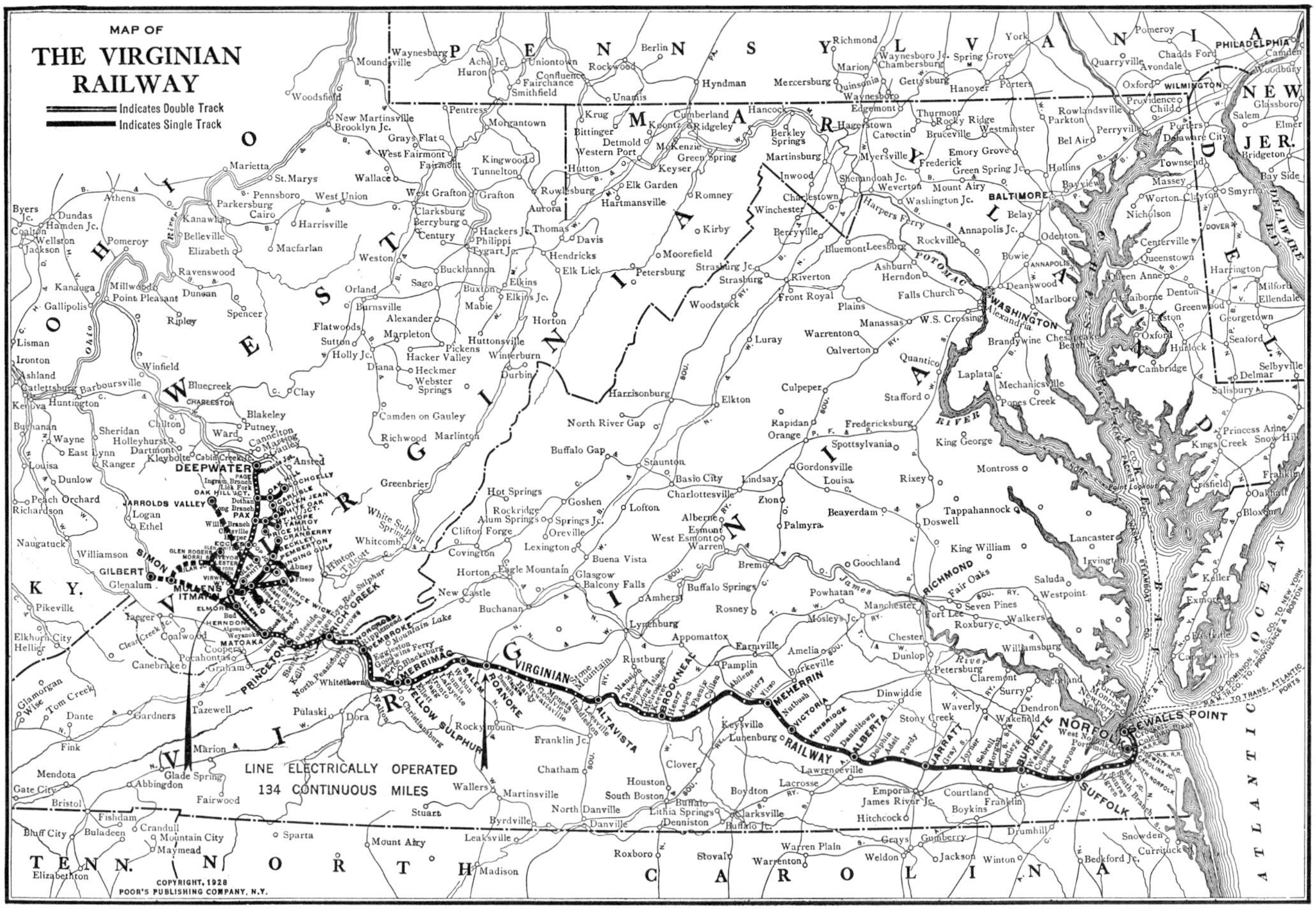

The Virginian Railway as it appeared in 1928 (from *Poor's Manual of the Railroads*). Unlike the C&O and N&W it had no western lines and was built strictly to compete with those two roads for tidewater coal business.

The Appalachian Plateau

Virginian 737 was built in 1919 as N&W Y-3 No. 2015 by the United States Railroad Administration. In 1943, the Santa Fe purchased 737 and seven other of her class for wartime service. In December 1947 the Santa Fe sold No. 737 to the Virginian, where it remained in mine-run service until its scrapping in 1955. In this photo 737 is at Pineville, West Virginia, in the late summer of 1952, along the Guyandotte River on a branch line which deserves more than the Deepwater line to be called the true main line of the Virginian.

H. Reid

H. Reid

In this portrait of a rebuilt United States Railroad Administration 2-8-8-2 at Elmore (August 1950), the front sand pipe shows prominently, leading from sand dome to second driver. One wonders where its flexible connection is!

H. Reid

Elmore Yard near Mullens, West Virginia, sits in a deep valley on the uppermost Guyandotte River. East of here is the climb to the top of the Plateau—namely, Great Flat Top Mountain at Clark's Gap. This engine terminal scene was made in August 1950.

At Elmore Yard (near Mullens), nestled in the high hills formed by the steady upward slope of the Appalachian Plateau, one found electric locomotives for the climb up and out of the Plateau and steamers for winding through the "hollows" searching for coal mines. In this August 1952 scene, two former C&O 0-8-0s (retaining same numbers) share attention with a USRA 2-8-8-2.

H. Reid

Between the end of World War II and 1949 were glory days at Elmore assembly yards, tucked in the remote hills of Wyoming County, at the base of Flat Top Mountain. Then one could have seen America's only extant 2-10-10-2s as well as 2-8-8-2s, 2-8-2s, the world's largest electrics and this remnant of the Virginian Triplex 2-8-8-8-4 No. 700, which was first a 2-8-8-0 before a trailing truck was added. That's a big boiler on this 2-8-8-2, No. 610! It's four inches higher overall than the Blue Ridge type 2-6-6-6 (the C&O called its 2-6-6-6s Allegheny and the Virginian locomotives, which were virtual duplicates of the C&O's, were called Blue Ridges.)

Gene Huddleston

The USRA-designed 2-8-8-2, being the standard mine-run locomotive on the Virginian, was found almost exclusively in the Appalachian Plateau, where most coal deposits were located. At the Elmore assembly yard, former N&W USRA Mallet 740 (ex-N&W 2026) reposes in the hazy sun of August 1949. In a four-year wartime stint on the Santa Fe, 740 had been numbered 1793.

H. Reid

55

"Tater Hill" dominates the town of Mullens in the background, and in the foreground, at the extreme western end of electrified territory, are "motors" and FM Trainmaster road switchers (2400 hp., purchased 1954 and 1957) awaiting servicing at the Mullens shops. Electrification would end two years later in 1962.

Gene Huddleston

Until 1954 one could view many kinds of steam and electric locomotives at the east end of Elmore Yard. The Guyandotte River, however, separated the yard from the highway and only a foot bridge connected the two. In 1957, the date of this photo, the "motors" of 1948 and 1956-57 were in service, although steam mostly had been gone since 1954.

Gene Huddleston

In 1959, just east of Elmore Yard, at the very bottom of the long grade leading out of the Guyandotte Valley to the top of the Plateau at Clark's Gap, a Fairbanks-Morse Trainmaster diesel road switcher heads upgrade with empty coal hoppers to supply nearby coal mines. The rectifier "motors" have come off the hill after shoving a coal train to the top.

Gene Huddleston

Two powerful ignition-recti-
fier "motors" wait at Elmore
Yards in September 1957 to
shove a drag to the top of the
Appalachian Plateau. These
EL-Cs, each rated at 3,300 hp.,
were less than one year old in
the fall of 1957. Seam of coal
visible in cut above the locomotives illustrates how rocks
in the uplifted plateau are
horizontal in bedding.

Gene Huddleston

Richard J. Cook

The Virginian, forced to climb to the top of the Appalachian Plateau to get through it, required five tunnels for the climb and eight bridges more than 100 feet long, including this curved trestle of 714 feet at Garwood, West Virginia. Pacific No. 213 is downgrade at 11:56 am, June 14, 1950 on passenger train No. 3.

Richard J. Cook

In the Virginian's 14-mile-long ascent of Flat Top Mountain spectacular bridges abound, including this one at Covel, West Virginia. "Squarehead" Electric No. 107 climbs eastward in June 1950 high above the valley of Gooney Otter Creek. A 100-ton capacity flat-bottom gondola is behind the locomotive.

H. Reid

Virginian Mikado No. 464 (class MC) switches at the storage yard in Princeton, West Virginia, July 29, 1953. Princeton is at the top of the Appalachian Plateau. The fact that Princeton was always headquarters for Virginian's New River Division explains the large building housing the depot and division offices in the background.

58

Enormous power was expended by the electric "motors" but they gave little auditory sign of it.

Richard J. Cook

Between Bluefield, West Virginia and Glen Lyn, Virginia on the New River, the Alleghany Front butts up against the Valley and Ridge section. Through the rift between the two sections the East River flows and N&W follows this rift in ascending the Plateau to Bluefield. (The Virginian follows the rift about halfway up toOakdale, West Virginia—then turns north to Princeton). Here Virginian "motor" 105 ascends the grade at Oakvale in 1956. N&W main behind cameraman.

Richard J. Cook

Dynamic braking on this three-unit, side-rod, box-cab electric helps control the speed of a coal train descending from the top of the Appalachian Plateau to the level of the New River via the "rift" valley of the East River in 1949. The westbound EL2-B at left, with empties, is in the passing siding. Here at Kellysville, West Virginia, the N&W mainline parallels the Virginian across the narrow valley.

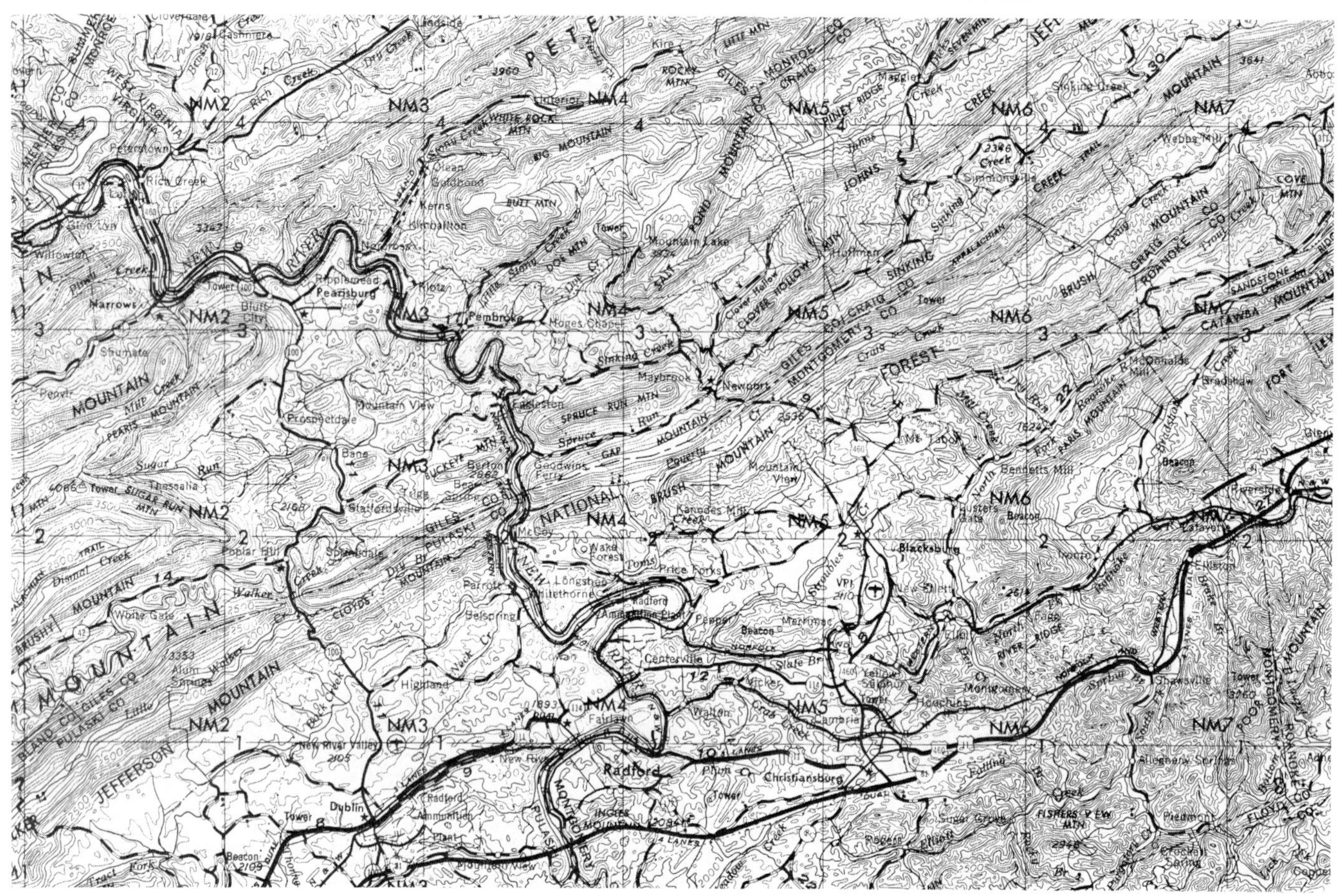

The main focus of map "E" is the Middle New River area between Glen Lyn to just north of Radford, Virginia. The N&W is on the west side of the river from Glen Lyn to the base of Alleghany Mountain at Walton. The Virginian, like the N&W, comes down the East River from on top of the Plateau to the level of the New at Glen Lyn. The Virginian, however, crosses the river from Glen Lyn to Rich Creek and runs on the east bank to the base of Alleghany Mountain across the New from Pepper. Plainly visible on the map are two great ridges the railroads and river cut through: Peters Mountain (east of New River) and East River Mountain (west of the river) and Big Walker Mountain (named so on both sides). The former ridge is gapped just west of the town of Narrows and the latter ridge between McCoy and Berton (Giles and Pulaski County line). Angel's Rest, atop Pearis Mountain, is southeast of Narrows. The summit of N&W's Allegheny grade is just north of Christiansburg and the summit of the old Virginian (labeled N&W on the map) is at the tunnel visible just south of Merrimac. A portion of the Great Valley shows in the extreme southeast corner of the map, and a portion of the Appalachian Plateau Province is in the extreme northwest corner. Most of the map is in the Valley and Ridge Province.

(VGN)

Glen Lyn. Where one province ends and the other begins. It's a place of unique beauty on the "middle" New River.

Richard J. Cook

At Glen Lyn, Virginia, just over the West Virginia state line, the Appalachian Plateau meets the Valley and Ridge Province. This westbound train of empties in 1953 climbs out of the New River Valley in its ascent of the Plateau. Behind the EL-2B "motors" are foothills associated with the big ridges of the Valley and Ridge Province.

Richard J. Cook

When the Virginian, under construction eastward late in 1907, reached the New River at Glen Lyn, the N&W (bottom of photo) already occupied the west bank, so there was no choice but to cross to the east bank, descending a 1.5 percent grade all the while. Both roads followed the river south to near Radford before leaving it. EL-2B "streamliner" No. 126, which developed a starting tractive effort of 260,000 pounds, is headed west June 12, 1956.

Most Virginian "squarehead" electrics were semi-permanently coupled as three-unit locomotives having only one number, like No. 108 descending into the New River Valley at Glen Lyn, Virginia, June 12, 1956 on its way to Roanoke. The huge mass of Peters Mountain is hidden from view, for the "Narrows", through which both N&W and Virginian pass, is several miles down the line.

Richard J. Cook

Here at Glen Lyn, the Plateau abuts the Ridge and Valley Province and behind the photographer the New cuts through the first of the great ridges at the appropriately named Narrows. Both the Virginian and N&W here descended from the top of the Plateau to river level before each followed the river on opposite banks. The degree of descent of this eastbound train in 1953 is not made apparent in the photo, for the bridge is at an oblique angle to the photographer, and thus the piers tend to look the same height.

Richard J. Cook

This photo was made 33 years after the striking photo of "motor", No. 103 by Richard Cook in 1953. On the morning Mr. Cook caught the eastbound coal train (above), fog obscured the mountain mass marking the Alleghany Front. This photo taken in 1986 from almost the same spot (looking north), shows not only high hills but the abandonment of the Virginian line, which followed by more than 10 years its merger into the N&W (now Norfolk Southern) in 1959.

Gene Huddleston

Valley and Ridge Province

Because the Virginian closely paralleled the Norfolk and Western through most of the Valley and Ridge Province, the photos of the two roads in the New River Valley southeast of Glen Lyn are placed together in the Norfolk and Western coverage.

This westbound train has just climbed Alleghany Mountain out of the Roanoke basin and is heading downgrade to the New River. The summit tunnel in the background, nearly a mile long, is the longest on the Virginian. The photographer is standing on the now-abandoned overpass of the N&W's Blacksburg branch. The time and place: Merrimac, Virginia, March 1958. The two class EL-C locomotives are a little over a year old.

Herbert H. Harwood, Jr.

Before the Virginian (or the Norfolk and Western) could leave the Valley and Ridge Province, they had to cross a divide between this province and the Great Valley. For the Virginian this divide involved a near-mile long tunnel.

The Great Valley
(The Shenandoah)

Gene Huddleston

In February 1948 an EL-2B "motor" leaves Roanoke, near the eastern edge of the Great Valley, westbound for Elmore, West Virginia. This manifest train will follow the banks of the Roanoke River for several miles, cross the N&W at Wabun (Singer) on the N&W, location of the painting of the back cover of this book and then begin to ascend to the summit of Alleghany Mountain in the Valley and Ridge Province.

This 1948 General Electric locomotive was about the last of its breed, for electrification from either overhead wires or a "third rail" became mostly outmoded by the rapid development of diesel-electric power following World War II. This EL-2B leaves Roanoke, February 1948.

Gene Huddleston

An EL-2B No. 126, brand new in February 1948, moves up from the Roanoke engine terminal to couple onto the west-bound time freight about 11 am. Both General Electric units, operated as a single locomotive, exert 6,800 hp. The train will follow the banks of the Roanoke River to Salem, where it will leave the Great Valley and start ascending the Alleghanies before descending to the New River, which cuts through the major ridges.

Gene Huddleston

The Blue Ridge

East of Roanoke, the Virginian passes through the Blue Ridge via an unscenic water gap, a combination of the Roanoke River and its tributary — Goose Creek. Perhaps the only scenic spot is just west of Huddleston Tunnel, where the railway crosses Goose Creek on a .6 percent grade and approaches Stone Mountain via curves of up to nearly 8 degrees. For whatever reason, few photos were taken in this area.